Reflections of a Cynical Clinical Psychologist

Presenting first-hand accounts from the 'front line', *Reflections of a Cynical Clinical Psychologist* provides the reader with a participant experience of the daily ups and downs of a US mental health professional. Vividly describing actual clinical events ranging from tragic to comedic, this book calls attention to the human realities of the system's dysfunction.

Illustrated throughout by anecdotes based on the author's 50 years of experience and observations in the field, the book focuses on 'the system' as the problem, identifying the limitations in current mental health policy with the emphasis misplaced on profit rather than optimal patient care. These anecdotes are organized by themes such as the harsh treatment of patients by staff; loss in the workplace; anomalous staff behavior; problems with the legal system; and clinically unexpected and bizarre episodes.

The value of humor as a stress reducer, social leveler and a means to make incisive points is highlighted throughout. This is important reading for mental health professionals, policy makers and those interested in humanizing social policy.

Max Heinrich, Ph.D., is a clinical psychologist who earned his Ph.D. from Cornell University in 1968. He has worked primarily with the seriously and persistently mentally ill in hospital settings. For most of that time he directed various inpatient and outpatient services. He has won local, state and national awards for public advocacy on behalf of his profession. Currently his week is divided between treating patients and teaching students on a psychiatric inpatient unit in a public hospital, as well as maintaining an extensive private practice.

Reflections of a Cynical Clinical Psychologist

Max Heinrich

Routledge
Taylor & Francis Group

LONDON AND NEW YORK

First published 2020
by Routledge
2 Park Square, Milton Park, Abingdon, Oxon OX14 4RN

and by Routledge
52 Vanderbilt Avenue, New York, NY 10017

Routledge is an imprint of the Taylor & Francis Group, an informa business

© 2020 Max Heinrich

British Library Cataloguing-in-Publication Data
A catalogue record for this book is available from
the British Library

Library of Congress Cataloging-in-Publication Data
Names: Heinrich, Max (Clinical psychologist), author.
Title: Reflections of a cynical clinical psychologist / Max Heinrich.
Description: Abingdon, Oxon ; New York, NY : Routledge, 2020. |
    Includes bibliographical references and index.
Identifiers: LCCN 2019055780 | ISBN 9780367336400 (hardback) |
    ISBN 9780367336394 (paperback) | ISBN 9780429320965
    (ebook)
Subjects: MESH: Mental Health Services—organization &
    administration | Psychology, Clinical—organization &
    administration | Quality of Health Care | Health Policy |
    United States | Personal Narrative
Classification: LCC RA790.53 | NLM WM 30 AA1 |
    DDC 362.2—dc23
LC record available at https://lccn.loc.gov/2019055780

ISBN: 978-0-367-33640-0 (hbk)
ISBN: 978-0-367-33639-4 (pbk)
ISBN: 978-0-429-32096-5 (ebk)

Typeset in Times New Roman
by Apex CoVantage, LLC

"If you want to tell people the truth, you'd better make them laugh, otherwise they'll kill you."

— G. B. Shaw*

"Men will always be mad, and those who think they can cure them are the maddest of all."

— Voltaire**

"Fellow citizens, we cannot escape history."

— Abraham Lincoln***

* 1951 October 13, The Saturday Review, Ideas on Film: Edinburgh's Documentary Festival by Cecile Starr, Start Page 60, Quote Page 60, Column 1, Saturday Review Associates, New York.
** Letter to Louise Dorothea of Meningen, *Duchess of Saxe-Gotha Madame*, January 30, 1762.
*** A. Lincoln, *Annual Message to Congress – Concluding Remarks*, Washington, DC, December 1, 1862.

In loving memory of my parents, Mildred and Charles

Contents

Acknowledgments

First and foremost, it is with heartfelt gratitude that I wish to acknowledge my wife Rae-ann for her invaluable editorial assistance. This book would not read as well, certainly not as coherently, had I not had her input and support all along the way.

To my family and many friends and colleagues who read or listened to all or parts of the numerous drafts of this work, thank you for your time, your suggestions and your support.

I would also like to express my appreciation to all those mentioned herein (anonymously of course) who in one way or another provided me with such an exciting and meaningful career.

Introduction

As a clinical psychologist in practice for over half a century, I have borne witness to an increasingly dysfunctional mental health system. Historically problematic, it has steadily morphed into a corrosive business archetype where treatment, once our fundamental mission, has become purely incidental to profit, where minimizing cost, rather than meeting human needs, is what matters most.

Part chronicle, part commentary, often sad, sometimes just comic relief, the insights I write about reflect my personal and professional struggles in this malfunctioning system. The underlying frustration and consequent anger I feel will be obvious to the reader yet I hope I have buffered this somewhat through my use of humor. The comedy intrinsic in many of these anecdotes is often dark, but it has helped me maintain a balanced view in difficult situations given my penchant for employing humor when trying to understand and defend against the often absurd, illogical and contradictory nature of both social policy and professional interpersonal interactions.

In *The Joker: A Memoir* by Andrew Hudgins,[1] he pointed out that humor "illuminate(s) the irresolvable contradictions our lives are built on." Lawrence J. Epstein,[2] in his book *The Haunted Smile: A Story of Jewish Comedians in America*, commented that over the centuries Jews have used humor defensively. For me it has been a necessary shield as I continued my work in increasingly rigid and dehumanizing institutions. Overall, while this account is cynical and even grim at times, in no way do I mean to discount the many gratifying and fulfilling experiences I have had along the way, nor the satisfaction of knowing that in spite of it all, many in need have been helped.

During her treatment one day, a patient told me she had been in and out of mental hospitals her whole adult life. I immediately realized that this was essentially true for me as well, and therein lies a tale.

Notes

1 A. Hudgins, *The Joker: A Memoir*, New York, NY: Simon and Schuster, 2013.
2 L. J. Epstein, *The Haunted Smile, A Story of Jewish Comedians in America*, New York, NY: Public Affairs, Perseus Books Group, 2001.

Part I

Institutions

Chapter 1

Graduate school

Prologue to hypocrisy

Graduate school was my first introduction to the arbitrary treatment of the mentally ill. I recall a rather hefty, bull-necked professor of psychology who frequently punctuated his lectures with pejorative remarks about psychiatry and clinical psychology. Referring to these disciplines as "fraudulent", he would rail on and on, continually deriding the clinically applied disciplines of the behavioral sciences.

One fall afternoon this professor walked into class and taught what seemed to be all of the rest of the semester's work. Then he walked out without another word.

A day or so later, while sitting in the student union cafeteria, I chanced upon a newspaper article of local interest: A woman had been caught speeding on a highway near campus. She was pulled over by the police but when asked for her license, she immediately sped off. The police followed in hot pursuit. The driver was clocked at speeds well over 100 miles per hour and was finally apprehended at a roadblock in town. The police ordered the driver out of the car whereupon out stepped my statistics professor wearing a dress and wig. He was jailed overnight and released on the stipulation that he obtain psychiatric treatment. Despite my attempts, as well as those of other graduate students, to point out that having what was then considered a psychiatric disorder should not automatically be a basis for dismissal from a faculty position, especially in the psychology department, our professor was nevertheless forced to resign from the university. Apparently he was not alone within the department in his contempt for the value of psychotherapeutic treatment.

Sadly this professor was not the last mental health professional I would witness being summarily terminated as a result of a behavioral disorder. This was prologue to the hypocrisy I would eventually come to recognize as pervasive in the mental health field.

Clinical encounters

In the 1960s, people with mild intellectual impairment were technically (and unsympathetically) dismissed as "Morons". Moderately impaired individuals were labeled Imbeciles, and those with severe mental retardation were classified as Idiots. These labels were all based on specific standardized IQ ranges. Perhaps this moralistically tinged nomenclature was a reflection of the poor technical understanding of these disorders at that time.

One of my assignments as a graduate student was to travel to what was then called a state training school where the 'mentally retarded' were tucked away from public view. My task was to administer the legally required annual routine intelligence tests to confirm the inmates' low IQ scores for the purpose of justifying their continued, essentially involuntary inpatient status. A more accurate designation for this institution might have been state 'maintenance' school as the residents remained there indefinitely and, despite the reference to 'training', none was evident.

On one ward there were rooms filled with net-covered cribs, essentially cages, inside of which were human beings of all sizes, with all manner of deformities. Most had abnormally small or large heads, and fixed stares and were lying in more or less frozen positions. On the ceiling was a flashing, revolving yellow light and when I asked a nurse what that was, her answer was very unsettling: "Oh, that's their entertainment!"

On another ward I examined a young woman in her 20s. Her test results indicated she was of low average intelligence with many behaviors more consistent with a diagnosis of schizophrenia than mental retardation. When I presented my findings to my supervisor, along with the suggestion that she be appropriately transferred, he gently told me that given the comparative quality of life in her current setting versus the state hospital to which she would inevitably be sent, it was probably in her best interest to leave her where she was. This admired and trusted supervisor was making the most humane judgment he could in the face of an overall inhumane system.

An embarrassing incident occurred when a group of us were traveling by bus to this institution. During the ride an intern colleague and I had made several mental retardation 'jokes', to the apparent delight of our fellow students and, as we pulled up to the parking area, we were all smiles. As we began to disembark, however, one of the women in our party ever so casually, but perhaps with an edge of hostility, mentioned that while she was here she would be visiting her sister, a resident. In retrospect I realized she had not been laughing at our 'jokes'.

A hard lesson was thus learned about sensitivity concerning this very real kind of tragedy and its impact on the family, as well as the need to practice better discretion around those you don't know well.

Chapter 2

The city hospital

Training wreck

Any remaining expectation of humanistic or even rational treatment for defenseless human beings, in this case psychiatric patients, was swept away by the various training experiences I was now being paid for.

In the city hospital where I interned, as well as the other settings in which my training took place, most of the patients came from impoverished and disorganized communities. They languished on locked wards for varying periods of time, dressed only in standard issue hospital gowns of uniform pattern and color, open at the back. The physicians who treated them were well dressed and preoccupied primarily with going on to (or were already attending) psychoanalytic institutes so eventually they could treat wealthy individuals in their private practices. The administration of maximal amounts of medication along with minimal amounts of humanity was their apparent treatment philosophy.

The doors to these wards were kept locked and the keys were of substantial size and weight. The furniture was heavy Mission Oak, the kind only the strongest patients could throw at you. The only eating utensils provided were spoons. And, as if patients were not humiliated enough by the admission and evaluation procedures, their belts and shoelaces were immediately confiscated so they would not be able to hang themselves, never mind that sheets and towels were always handy for this method of escape. Is it really possible to hang yourself with shoelaces? ("Breakaway" shoelaces and "breakaway belts", possibly even edible, providing late night snacks when the staff was asleep, might become a big seller if anyone cared to do the research, development and subsequent marketing. The sales pitch could be: "Better laced than never!")

The chief psychologist at this city hospital, a particularly brilliant man, was rumored to have such a clear view of reality that he was chronically depressed as a result. He would often conduct interviews with patients, usually ones with severe diagnoses such as schizophrenia, in the presence of the entire psychology department, ostensibly for teaching purposes. Invariably he would conclude these examinations with a series of increasingly complex proverbs, the patients struggling to discern the meaning while growing more and more uncomfortable and confounded by the sheer abstruseness of these aphorisms. An example: If you're going to sup with the devil, bring a long spoon.

After the patients were taken away, this chief would turn to us and declare that the progressive bafflement evidenced by the patients was consistent with a thought disorder, one associated with their particular psychiatric diagnosis. The staff kept it secret from the chief that often these same proverbs baffled us!

What follows are three scenarios (true enough) to capture the overall anomic essence of the city hospital in the early 1960s.

Scene 1 – A bare hospital room containing four beds, each with its own dented, sharp edged metal bedside stand painted white. The enameled beds with their iron pipe-like foot- and headboards are also painted white. The sheets and blankets are white. The plaster walls are covered with thick layers of fissured white paint. The nurses, doctors and orderlies all wear white. The complexions of the bedded patients range from pale to very pale. (The hospital staff doesn't look much better.) The surfaces are hard. Noises are distant and muffled. Light, filtered by uneven layers of dust and grime, comes from two sources: through large uncurtained windows and also radiating from globes suspended from the high ceilings, casting unpleasant shadows. Every surface, animate and inanimate, reflects this light. It is as if all color and sound have been drained from the world. The patients lie still, flat on their backs, their breathing barely discernible. Their only possible entertainment, rarely interrupted by hospital staff or procedures, is the view of endless designs in the myriad cracks and shadows on the walls and ceiling. There are no TV's, no radios, few visitors, no volunteers bringing good cheer, companionship, books or magazines. This was a charity ward for the elderly mentally ill at a time when they were referred to as the 'aged'. It was truly an ancient city hospital, often the final resting place before the final resting place.

One patient, with a great view of the ceiling, is lying especially still in his bed. An orderly, at that time a position requiring very little training, enters the room and immediately recognizes the patient is dead because there are two untouched glasses of orange juice on his bedside table! One can imagine the doctor coming in to pronounce him "unjuiced"!

Scene 2 – An escort has been called to the emergency department where a nurse orders him to transport a critically ill patient to the Intensive Care Unit (ICU). The escort wheels the patient on a gurney toward the elevator and, after the requisite patience-challenging wait, the elevator eventually comes and they enter. The doors close, the floor button is pushed, and the patient dies. Despite the apparent death, the escort delivers the body to the ICU where a nurse takes one look and asks the escort, "Where do you think you're going with 'that'?" The escort makes an attempt to explain but as he opens his mouth, the nurse curtly orders him out of the ICU stating, "We don't accept dead bodies here!" The escort heads back to the emergency department to return the body. When he greets the original nurse with the news, without even verifying the accuracy of the escort's statement, the nurse immediately orders him out of the ER with the body. "He was alive when he left here, and that's all I know," she says. Intimidated by her hyper-authority, the escort retreats with the body.

A few days later a security guard finds it on a sun porch.

Scene 3 – The hospital pharmacy, long lines of people waiting to have prescriptions filled. There is no separate window for staff at this institution; they just cut right to the front. On this day, however, no pharmacist is behind the window. Assuming he or she has gone to retrieve a medication for the next person in line, an intern waits, five minutes, ten minutes, before finally stepping over to the other window and making the obvious inquiry as to the whereabouts of the first pharmacist. Clarification is finally achieved: "Oh, he went to lunch." No announcement, no sign. No problem. Just many 'insignificant' people left standing there for the entirety of the pharmacist's lunch hour.

Case conferences

The conduct of interdisciplinary case conferences on one of the locked inpatient units provides insight into the dehumanizing ambience in the hospital. Picture the staff, seated around three sides of a rectangular oak table leaving the fourth side empty. Wearing the typical hospital gown, open at the back (thus exposing his or her posterior), the patient is then ushered in and told to *stand* at the vacant end. A series of very personal questions is asked by one of the doctors, along with comments from the staff, almost as if the intent is to humiliate the patient: "So, Mr. S, are you still involved with those farm animals?" Okay, an exaggeration, after all we were in the city!

Prior to these case conferences, the psychology interns were allotted a mere 15 minutes during which to examine the patient and collect sufficient information to present a preliminary psychological overview. A psychological assessment generally takes a few hours before a reasonably accurate diagnostic impression can be arrived at yet, oddly enough given the intense focus required during these seemingly surreal exams, more often than not the necessary complete follow-up examination confirmed we had indeed captured the essence of the patient's dysfunctional behavior in those few minutes. Certainly the value of paying very close attention was driven home and, in this instance, at very high speed.

Clinical rotations

During my internship, I rotated through five different services, each experience lasting ten weeks. I always worked under supervision yet it was clear there would be heavy reliance on my assessments and recommendations. For example, on a medical unit I evaluated a male patient in his early 40s with a diagnosis of severe stomach ulceration. What distinguished this patient from the usual diagnostic referrals I saw was the utterly profound impact my clinical judgment would have: If I determined this patient could follow a very strict and somewhat complicated diet, he would avoid having to undergo major abdominal surgery for removal of his stomach. From their appraisal of the patient's mental status, the surgeons suspected he lacked sufficient intelligence to sustain compliance with the more conservative dietary treatment approach, but their ultimate decision would be based on my definitive recommendation after examination. Dutifully I conducted the exam, carefully evaluated the data and prudently made the painful judgment. The patient's stomach was removed. This experience amplified the reality of my work.

During my rotation to the Prison Ward, what today would be called the *Forensic Unit*, the first patient I saw was a man who had killed another man for making a homosexual pass at him in a public bathroom. My task, under supervision, was to determine if this prisoner could comprehend the nature of the charge against him and assist counsel in his defense. If he could not, as turned out to be the case, he would be transferred to the state hospital for the criminally insane for 'treatment' until he was capable of defending himself in court, a rare outcome.

Another inmate recently admitted to this Prison Ward was a slightly effeminate black male in his 30s, charged with mugging another man. His modus operandi was to dress up as a woman and lure unsuspecting 'johns' into what they thought was going to be a sexual moment and then attack them. His intake interview was conducted by a psychiatrist and yielded some surprises: The prisoner explained that he occasionally supplemented his income by allowing men to have anal intercourse with him. Interested in the clinical implications of this new information, the psychiatrist inquired whether the prisoner ever performed anal intercourse on these 'johns'. "What, are you crazy? That's sick! I would never do that," the prisoner indignantly exclaimed. He was so put off by what he considered the psychiatrist's "inappropriate" remarks that he insisted the interview be immediately terminated.

During my assignment to the state penitentiary, a paradoxical yet instructive experience occurred. In preparation for his upcoming parole board hearing, I examined an inmate imprisoned (at least for the second time) for check forgery. He was a friendly man but showed little, if any, helpful findings on the exam with regard to his readiness for parole. He finally confessed he didn't really want to leave prison. He had no family and no ties to the outside community. In prison he lived in a minimum-security section, he wrote for the prison newspaper and he played on the prison baseball team. He had found a home and a community here and, except for the lack of women, he said this was the perfect place for him.

Over the years I would encounter many such institutionalized individuals whose solution to loneliness was to sustain, or at least report as such, their symptoms of mental illness. Society's inadequate response to the needs of these people continues even today.

On the Psychiatric Outpatient Service, I treated a nice-looking, middle-aged African-American male with a chief complaint of alcoholism. He appeared very sad, obviously depressed and weighed down by a great deal of personal baggage. Although he claimed he had not been drinking for a long while, he left the precise length of time undefined.

The patient described a rather unsettled, bittersweet childhood that he seemed to realize was at the core of his present difficulties. Raised by white foster parents, he had believed himself to be white until, at about the age of 13, a series of racial slurs directed at him shocked him into the awareness that he was black. This was something he continued to find difficult to accept.

What I'll probably never forget was his fixation on his saddle shoes. A fashion staple of the time, saddle shoes were white leather shoes with brown (or black) 'saddles' sewn over the instep areas of the shoes, leaving the heel and toe areas bright white. During his therapy, the patient repeatedly returned to the theme of his difficulty in keeping his shoes properly polished. "The white polish keeps getting on the brown and the brown polish keeps getting on the white," he would complain, over and over again. Despite modest gains made in his treatment, he never fully understood the symbolic racial identity confusion likely reflected in this obsession over his shoes. Fortunately for him, saddle shoes became far less popular soon afterward.

When his treatment was terminated after three months, the patient claimed continued sobriety and significantly reduced depression, along with improved self-esteem. Never before, nor since, have I seen such definitive physical acting out of an unconscious conflict on a symbolic level with little, if any, substantial insight ever being achieved.

A rather memorable, histrionic moment occurred when I administered a Rorschach Inkblot Test[1] to a female on the inpatient psychiatric unit. When I presented a card to her, one commonly interpreted as two animals climbing up the sides of the blot, she suddenly and dramatically threw the card across the room and shouted, "Get those rats away from me!". Her uncritical and literal interpretation of what was essentially representational material, followed by her immediate impulsive and bizarre behavior, drove home for me the reality, pain and intensity of severe mental illness, in a new, experiential way.

Another psychiatric inpatient I evaluated suffered from Korsakoff's syndrome, a severe dementia related to Thiamine (Vitamin B1) deficiency, a consequence of lifelong alcohol abuse. During World War II he had served in the Army and after discharge worked in a factory packing goods. When asked his military rank, as part of his initial workup, he condensed those two experiences and answered, "Packer, First Class". On the unit he was often seen searching for the lavatory and repeatedly asking, "Where did they put that bathroom now?"

Sadly this patient was one of many who failed to receive adequate treatment.

On an inpatient medical unit I was given the challenging task of administering a psychological examination to a man paralyzed from the neck down after he had gone through the windshield of the truck he was driving. The purpose of the exam was to determine reasonable post-hospital vocational goals based on an assessment of the patient's cognitive skills.

The patient was lying face down on a Stryker frame,[2] so this was not easy. The frame was low to the ground and the patient obviously could not manage handling the test materials, thus narrowing my examination to only verbal measures. Not realizing the position of the frame could be changed, it occurred to me that if I had the use of one of those trolleys that auto mechanics lie on when repairing the undersides of vehicles, it might have been easier.

A rather morbid aspect of my training was the assigned observation of the weekly 'brain cutting' or, more accurately, 'slicing' that took place in the morgue, deep within the bowels of the hospital. The neuropathologist, always dressed informally in a checkered flannel shirt, would jovially slice up newly harvested human brains as if they were sides of roast beef, all the while discoursing on the physical findings of neuropathology. One brain I was shown belonged to a patient who died of tuberculosis; it appeared to be covered in a white powdery substance resembling talcum powder.

The most striking aspect of this morgue experience was learning that most, if not all human brains, even those of people who had died of non-neurological disorders, showed some evidence of neuropathology not necessarily manifest during life. I began to wonder about my own brain, especially in the quiet of the late night.

Curious, one day I picked up a paper shroud from a stack. My amused supervisor looked over and said, "Put that down, it's not your size!"

Supervision

The supervision we received as interns was not always what one might have expected. For example, when I questioned the theoretical validity of the psychoanalytic concept of the Oedipus complex,[3] my supervisor accused me of obviously having an unresolved one myself. Apparently her underlying assumption was that disagreement with psychoanalytic theory (known clinically as 'resistance') was proof of the theory's validity. This example of rigid, categorical conceptualization reminded me of a dispute Woody Allen once had with the Internal Revenue Service about deducting the cost of his psychoanalysis. He said: "I had formed a corporation and tried to take my analyst off as a business deduction. The government said it was entertainment. . . . We compromised finally and made it a religious contribution."[4]

When treating another patient suffering from alcohol related dementia, my supervisor insisted I tell him that if he drank *even one more time*, he would die. It is highly unlikely that one more episode of drinking would actually have resulted in such a dramatic outcome, and while this may have been a well-intentioned effort to get the patient to stop drinking, essentially it was disrespectful, dishonest and neither clinically accurate nor ethical.

Similarly, a supervisor once instructed me to tell a manipulative and suicidal patient she should give us sufficient notice of her next attempt so we could give her appointment to someone else. Essentially he wanted me to call her bluff but, considering it insensitive and unethical, I made a judgment not to follow this 'suggestion'.

During my rotation to the outpatient service, I treated a likeable young gay man who was fairly immature and self-centered. He was being 'kept' by an older man and thus had never needed to seek gainful employment. At the direction of my supervisor, I told the patient he should get a job, and soon thereafter he told me he had. However, two months later, he confessed he had lied to me; he hadn't even looked for one but was simply trying to please me. Maybe my supervisor's intent was to teach something about not telling people you are treating what to do since this creates the potential for dishonest interactions.

This particular lesson, if that's what it was intended to be, unfortunately was at the patient's expense.

Group psychotherapy

During my internship, learning to conduct group therapy turned out to be a matter of *not* accepting what I observed several supervisors doing, perhaps another example of teaching by the inverse. For example, in a psychotherapy group led by a psychologist and a psychiatrist, the patients were encouraged to talk about their problems and expose their dysfunctional selves to the group. One female patient continuously paced around the room in an agitated state. Obviously she did not want to be there but was forced to remain because the therapists had locked the door.

During the last ten minutes of the session, the two therapists systematically humiliated everyone in the room with moralistic interpretations of the information each of these so vulnerable patients had shared. Everyone, that is, except the woman who had said nothing.

Another group I participated in as a co-leader was conducted by a rather arrogant, insensitive psychologist whose abrupt, judgmental, unrelated and even elitist style of communication only seemed to make the patients feel worse about themselves. Here was yet another lesson in how *not* to do group psychotherapy.

Although the way to proceed was not always clear in these situations, the group experiences I learned the most from were the ones where I actually had no clinical supervisor. Once, thinking I was being therapeutically provocative in an outpatient group, I told a patient he was "boring me". His reply, a brilliant and instructive comeback, was that he was not there to entertain me! Here finally was a straightforward teacher.

In an inpatient group where I worked with a co-therapist, a number of participants insisted on calling us "doctor" despite the pains we took to remind them we were not yet doctors. Although they accepted that fact, they said it made them feel better to call us "doctor". This speaks to the awe inspired by physicians and the mystical powers often attributed to them by those desperate for caring and understanding. Physicians are often aided and abetted in this elitism by administrators. The deferential attitude of patients then supports the view of physicians that they are superior to other professionals, and this gives rise to the hierarchical structure in hospitals.

Throughout my career, I would face many forms of discrimination. For example, the chief psychologist in one hospital was the only non-physician permitted to eat in the doctor's dining room; no other psychologists or other mental health professionals were welcome. It is with some resentment that I recall that otherwise esteemed chief psychologist whose actions supported a policy that discriminated against his colleagues. As well, psychologists were not permitted to do individual psychotherapy, despite our well-established expertise in this procedure. The only exception was for the training of psychology interns.

Similar forms of bias in hospitals included the denial of medical staff membership, and admitting privileges to psychologists and other 'non-medical' professionals, the subordinating imposition of supervision by psychiatrists, few if any opportunities for promotion, and social event exclusions. Even such trivialities as restricted parking and lounge and gym privileges exist to this day.

While these slights may seem to be merely a matter of vanity, they represent much more. These hierarchical dividers impede communication, restrict program development and ultimately interfere with the optimal treatment of patients. The personal growth of staff is continually compromised by this counterproductive and divisive attitude, as they are constantly reminded they are only guests in the hospital and they should know their place and limitations. Thus, needless constraints are imposed on the optimally effective delivery of mental health services in our society.

Overall, however, in spite of the essentially dehumanizing atmosphere of the hospitals where I trained, my own experiences were actually excellent. Formative and lasting, life-changing, professional insights were gained. I recognized that the pernicious and persistent stressors associated with the low socio-economic status of a substantial segment of our population contributed significantly to the prevalence of mental illness. Painfully clear was the limited quantity and quality of treatment available then . . . and now.

Notes

1 H. Rorschach, *Rorschach Test*, 1927. Defined by Merriam-Webster as "a personality and intelligence test in which a subject interprets inkblot designs in
terms that reveal intellectual and emotional factors". Rorschach® is a regis-
tered trademark of Hogrefe AG – Bern, Switzerland.
2 A frame used to securely hold a patient in a fixed position; by turning the
frame, the patient's position can be changed from face up to face down, or
upright, without moving any individual parts of the body down thus minimizing skin breakdown.
3 According to Sigmund Freud, this is a crucial stage in a child's emotional
development with feelings of desire for the parent of the opposite sex and
jealousy and anger toward the parent of the same sex.
4 Allen, Woody, *The Stand Up Years 1964–1968*, New York, NY: Razor & Tie.
This Compilation: Earshot Music Publishing Co, Inc., Under exclusive license
to Razor & Tie Recordings, LLC. Marketed by Razor & Tie Recordings, 2014.

Chapter 3

The state hospital

The Willard Asylum for the Insane

My first full-time salaried position was at a facility then known as a 'state hospital', a world even more byzantine and bizarre than that of my internship at a 'city hospital'. Built in the mid-19th century, on the shores of a large lake in a very rural area, this complex of buildings was initially and formally termed a 'lunatic asylum'. Later it became known as a 'state hospital', and more recently as a 'psychiatric center', demonstrating the euphemistic progression of mental health nomenclature.

Approximately 3,000 patients were housed at this institution. The average length of stay was about 30 years. One could look at any of the patients' medical records, written by generations of nurses always with perfect flowing penmanship, and read such accounts as: "Leeches were applied today." One patient, a typhoid carrier admitted in 1896 (not a typo!), had been kept in isolation most of the time. Late in life she was given a television set and one had to wonder what anything she watched on that TV could have meant to her.

There were numerous back wards ("backwards" would be an ironic typo here) located in many of the buildings across the far-flung campus but only one physician per 600 patients. The acute care admissions center was fairly modern, but many of the other buildings had fallen into disuse despite the substantial patient census. One particularly large abandoned building was representative of the interior design of state hospitals at the time. Its entire first floor had been a Day Room reaching almost as far as the eye could see, seemingly having its own horizon. What was remarkable, even astonishing about this room was that upon entering, when you stepped on the maple floor, the wood crackled under your feet, the sound spreading wave-like outwards across its vast space. "A hundred years of urination by generations of mentally ill men have desiccated the floors resulting in this effect," offered the sage hospital elder who was showing me around.

Overlooking the lake was a French Empire style building no longer used as a facility for housing patients. Administrative offices were located on the first floor, and in the catacomb-like basement was a dining room for professional staff only, where lunch was served by uniformed waitresses.

Endless debates on the Vietnam War took place in that dining room, and a Catholic priest routinely denounced any opposition to the war. The head of building maintenance branded those of us against the war as "traitors" to our country, somewhat disingenuous considering he was a man who had earlier acknowledged his own arrest and conviction for unspecified war crimes during World War II.

Like many of the patients, the director of this institution (and several of the doctors) also had a length of stay of more than 30 years. He lived in a mansion on campus, attended by his patient-servants. The director of the medical hospital was legally blind. The consulting neurologist's automobile had multiple dents on both sides, her driving apparently matching her unsteady gait. Few (if any) of the 'psychiatrists' were actually licensed physicians, and one day we discovered that one had actually been a dentist in Europe! The majority of these 'psychiatrists' had Hispanic sounding last names but spoke with a hint of a German accent, suggesting they had spent time in South America recuperating from their 'service' in World War II. There were even rumors that surgical residents from a nearby residency training program practiced cholecystectomies (gall bladder removal surgery) on randomly selected patients.

The hospital had its own morgue, a small, one-story, dirty red brick building erected in the 1860s. Surrounded by wild, densely overgrown foliage, the only entrance was a faded, slightly warped wooden door badly in need of paint. One day the hospital's Protestant chaplain suggested I join him for lunch, as he often did. "But," he said, "First I have to stop at the morgue to do a funeral. It won't take long. An elderly patient died last night and is on her way to a medical school to serve as a cadaver." (After all, she did owe the state a favor as they had fed, clothed and boarded her for approximately most of her life while confining her to this hospital, so it was the least she could do!) Never having seen a Protestant funeral service, the idea was not at all inconvenient and even seemed intriguing, despite my intense hunger.

On that cold, nasty, overcast day the morgue building was a particularly unnerving sight and, with its peculiar musty smell, the overall effect was of having stepped into a three-dimensional horror film. As the chaplain and I entered the single room, this place of next-to-final rest, the first sound we heard was a continuous "put-put, chug-a-chug". That was the ancient refrigeration unit. (In an earlier time, half the room would probably have been filled with blocks of ice.) Standing hesitantly in the doorway, I noted a grouping of large oak drawers to my left, three rows with three drawers in each, set into an oak wall. These apparently were where the bodies were stored. Set back, off to my right and parallel to the structure with the drawers, was a massive, antique maple dissection/autopsy table. (Sanded and refinished, today it would make a nifty piece of furniture for some high-end apartment.) Resting on this table were a pile of toe tags, a stack of plastic shrouds, (remembering a previous shroud moment I didn't pick any of them up) and, inexplicably, a wooden mallet. (In case someone woke up?)

Before I could completely absorb the moment, more sounds were heard: Rung-a-dung dung dung! Rung-a-dung dung dung! "Where the hell is she?" the chaplain bellowed, furiously sliding drawers open and closed, looking for the deceased woman. (He was *really* hungry. I on the other hand had completely lost my appetite by this time.) Finally he slid out the bottom center drawer revealing a human body, wrapped and sort of bound in a white plastic shroud. "Here she is," he said with obvious satisfaction. With his back to me, facing the deceased he immediately launched into a series of what I assumed were Protestant prayers for the dead. Speaking in a rapid and matter-of-fact monotone, suggesting that he had no real feeling for this woman's life and death, he completed the 'microwave' or, better yet, 'drive-through' 'funeral service' with one "Amen". No 'Amen-arrhea'* here! Then, with more a sigh of personal relief than an expression of reverence, he put his foot on the top edge of the drawer and, using the full force of his leg, pushed it closed with one motion. Gedung!!!!! He turned and, finally showing some genuine emotion said, "Lunch?"

A curious characteristic about this particular chaplain was that he always wore a light gray suit and, although he worked full time at a state hospital, he drove a relatively new Cadillac. Whenever he approached his car dressed in that gray suit, he invariably gave the impression of being the chauffeur. There were many times when several of us would ride in the back seat while he drove and we found this seemingly dissonant idea endlessly amusing.

The hospital also had its own police force, fire department and sewage treatment plant, as well as its own morgue and its own cemetery. When patients died, they were buried in graves marked only with a number,

* Excessive prayer ending.

most having long since been abandoned and forgotten by their families. (Alternatively, the corpses might be sent to medical schools, no markers required.)

The man whose job it was to dig and care for those graves was a patient who had been admitted in 1918 and had spent most of his existence as a patient in this hospital, "the last several decades of his life on no medication"[1] with the implication that his illness may have been in remission. He died in 1968 at the age of 90. "He dug until he died . . . at least 15,000 graves, 60 to a row."[2] I can recall watching him, with a mixture of admiration and sadness, as he walked up the hill to the cemetery.

Around 2014 a project was begun to try to identify these deceased and properly mark their graves[3] thus finally providing them with some dignity. Unfortunately, efforts to restore those lost names were frustrated when the state initially withheld records claiming confidentiality. More recently, however, they agreed to attempt to secure permission from patients' families to allow identifying markers ("nearly 5,800") to be placed. Sadly, many records were actually lost.

An Associated Press bulletin demonstrated how the warehousing of patients, even in death, was universally widespread:

> They were dubbed the "forgotten souls" – the cremated remains of thousands of people who came through the doors of Oregon State Mental Hospital, died there and their ashes were abandoned inside 3,500 copper urns. Discovered a decade ago at the decrepit Oregon State Hospital, the remains became a symbol of the state's – and the nation's – dark history of treating the mentally ill.[4]

One of my early teaching experiences at this institution involved being asked to present a lecture to a class of about 50 nurses and attendants on some long forgotten mental health topic. The entire class stood as I walked into the large room, ethics and convention of the time requiring that non-professional staff (including nurses) stand when a professional (physician, psychiatrist, psychologist) entered the room. I was unprepared by any previous institutional experience for this seemingly 19th-century custom and immediately scrapped my planned lecture. Instead, I launched into a 'socio-historico-politico' analysis of what they had just done, suggesting that this deferential, demeaning custom was (one more example here of the previously discussed) unnecessary and destructive sustaining of hierarchical staff distinctions within the hospital. Those in the room seemed to understand and approve of my supportive comments, recognizing I was not a 'stand-up' guy.

No reference was ever made to this 'talk' by any hospital leadership or supervisor even though some were present at the time. Perhaps there was already some implicit realization that this quaint custom was part of a bygone era, and while it may not have 'sat' well with them, no move had yet been made to end it.

Then came the day when an olive drab amphibious landing craft suddenly appeared in front of the hospital's fire department building. (These were the "boats" from which our soldiers poured to storm the beaches in those WWII movies and newsreels shown in theaters at that time.) It was enormous, much larger than one would ever have imagined from the vantage point of a movie theater seat. The question was: What was it doing here at this hospital?

"Ah, that's obvious," one of the proud workmen said. The National Guard had donated it to enable the hospital staff to more efficiently retrieve the three or so bodies, on average, of patients who annually excursed into the lake. The fact that there were already at least 20 private boats tied up at the hospital's dock, any of which could be pressed into service for this almost always futile exercise, didn't seem to matter. This amphibious landing craft was presumed to be the quintessential piece of hospital equipment for retrieving the dead and/or the very wet mentally ill.

The proud maintenance staff, ironically under the direction of the WWII criminal previously mentioned, immediately painted it the state colors. (Unlike state universities, state hospitals apparently didn't have their own colors.) They fussed over their new acquisition with the glow and excitement of teenagers washing their first cars. Then they repossessed an old power plant on the grounds and modified it into a garage to protect their new vehicle from the elements. In doing so, they consumed the entire allotment of concrete for that year. And it was only spring!

Here's why the loss of that cement merits mention. Some 300 female psychiatric patients, housed in a building with only the most basic amenities, were awaiting the warmer weather for the promised installation of an outdoor barbecue facility so they could experience grilled hot dogs on Saturday afternoons, probably for the first time in their lives. To illustrate what this meant to those women, let me recount what their day-to-day lives were like.

Each of the large rooms in their building contained numerous beds. They took gang showers, wore simple hospital clothing and ate overcooked, high-carbohydrate institutional food. Their sheets, pillowcases and all the furniture were white (recall the city hospital referenced earlier). (A 'major advance' in mental health was made the day 'blankets of color' were introduced to break the mind-numbing visual monotony.) Among other precautions in place, and for reasons never made clear, even the toilet seats had been removed (or possibly never installed) although these were elderly women hardly able to, nor interested in vandalizing such items. There was only one physician and one social worker to supervise their care. The small number of devoted attendants could provide little beyond basic maintenance for the patients. There were virtually no activities, no diversions of any kind, simply nothing to do. An anomaly produced by overall staffing insufficiencies was that patients were routinely put to bed around 6:30 PM as the safest procedure available. Imagine the routine high doses of anti-psychotic and tranquilizing medications this must have required. Under those circumstances, the forfeiture of that allotment of barbecue cement was a great disappointment, not only to the patients but also to the staff who attended them. The loss of an anticipated weekly hot dog was no trivial matter in a life punctuated primarily by bedtimes. So, what to do?

Enter an assistant occupational therapist (OT) and a senior clinical psychologist (me). It just so happened that this assistant OT's father owned a hardware store a few miles from the hospital and, as fortune would have it, both he and I had enough practice with home repairs to embolden us to think we could attain, or possibly even exceed the same construction standards as the more experienced hospital maintenance staff. So, on a quiet Saturday morning, we set out on our semi-covert mission. We picked up two bags of ready-mix concrete and made our way back to the hospital grounds, unsure if our mission, if ever discovered, would be acceptable to the perpetually phantom director of the hospital. Watching for security patrols, we surreptitiously dug the requisite hole, mixed the cement, poured it, set in the vertical pipe on which the barbecue grill would sit, and held it in place until the mix sufficiently hardened and began to cure. (This was likely the only cure that ever took place in this hospital!)

With sustained 'covertion' we successfully completed our mission and, later that day, the ladies had their first hot dogs. It was clear to me that no pharmaceutical high could ever compare with the satisfaction of this experience, not only for the patients but for the staff as well. For the rest of my tenure at the state hospital, and to the best of my knowledge thereafter, the amphibious landing craft, voracious consumer of that year's cement allotment, was never pressed into the service for which it was intended.

While en route to a meeting with a social worker one day, we came upon about 40 women sitting on hard oak seats watching a black and white television mounted on a shoulder height platform. The vertical adjustment (remember that?) was off and the picture was rolling at sufficient speed to make the images incomprehensible. No one would have surmised that, however, from the intensity with which the women were watching the screen. Noticing the problem, the social worker went to the front of the room and adjusted the picture so it was sufficiently stable to enable comprehension. The patients actually applauded.

Aware of the profound lack of stimulation these female patients experienced in their daily lives on those back wards, I organized a group of fine arts students from a local college to paint murals in the halls, simple familiar images. Apparently I was not emphatic enough in my direction to the students as they chose to maintain their current academic focus on abstract art, probably as a matter of (narcissistic) principle. When the director of the hospital saw the "art work" he immediately became a critic. Subordinates quoted him (he never spoke to the staff directly) as saying, "If my patients are not going to have good art, they'll have no art at all." He had the murals painted over, restoring the original beige color of those walls. Imagine 300 chronically ill women with nowhere to go and nothing to do but stare at beige walls, day after day, for 30 years.

A colleague once observed a patient on the back wards whose skin was totally purple. When he asked one of the regular staffers, "What's with the purple guy?" the staffer responded, "What purple guy?" Upon further exploration it turned out that this African-American man, with the kind of very dark skin in which you might see a purple hue, had been started on Thorazine[5] (chlorpromazine) ten years earlier. The continued high doses of this drug had affected the melanin in his skin, slowly and gradually turning him completely purple. This side effect had occurred so insidiously that the day-to-day staff never noticed the change. This was a striking example of the kind of mechanical administration of medication to sustain behavioral control in spite of progressive long-term negative effects, so characteristic of state hospitals in the 1960s.

On one occasion I was part of a team evaluating female patients housed on a "violent" back ward. I was asked to examine a woman who had been kept in continual seclusion in a strait jacket in order to control what were referred to as her chronic "outbursts". The patient was unresponsive to any type of psychological examination but, after reading her chart, I formed a speculation that became the basis of my recommendation. I offered that perhaps she had a seizure disorder superimposed on her apparent psychosis and the high doses of Thorazine (2500 mg/day) might be lowering her seizure threshold thus potentiating her "outbursts". Surprisingly, the doctor actually readjusted her medication in light of my recommendation and she could soon be transferred to a regular back ward where, hopefully, she received a somewhat higher level of humane treatment.

I remember a routine case conference where an elderly woman was presented. Her initial complaint had been visual hallucinations as a result, she said, of taking the drug LSD,[6] all the rage at the time. The treatment plan was observation until the drug was eliminated from her body. Eventually, however, after more careful examination by one of the (few) actually knowledgeable psychiatrists on staff, it turned out the patient had read an article in *Life Magazine* that stated LSD caused visual hallucinations; since she was indeed having visual hallucinations she concluded she must have taken LSD. In essence, she had the delusion her hallucinations were LSD-induced. The psychiatrist concluded she was "obviously" schizophrenic, a diagnosis that might have been immediately apparent had a more careful initial examination been performed which would have led to timely treatment with appropriate medication. Clearly this was a case where treatment delayed was treatment denied.[7]

Electroconvulsive Therapy, commonly known as ECT, was a standard and routine component of the 'therapeutic' regimen for many of these patients, often regardless of their formal diagnoses. Unlike today's minimalist application of this modality, it was then rather barbaric. I once asked an attending psychiatrist how this treatment worked; "It straightens out the 'engrams' in the brain," he told me, as if that explained anything. (Engrams have been characterized as a hypothetical change in neural tissue that may account for the persistence of memory but the relationship of this concept to improvement after ECT remains enigmatic.) To this day, the exact mechanism of action of ECT is not well understood. Of course, if it were evidence-based, it might be called: DBT, Dielectrical Behavioral Treatment.[8]

Use of ECT in that institution was strictly a matter of staff judgment; it required no informed consent and was essentially involuntary. Treatments were usually applied serially to many patients at a designated time. The 'chosen' were lined up in the hall outside the ECT Room where they remained standing until it was their turn. Each patient was successively called into the room, placed on the table and held down by at least two attendants using pillows. A plastic airway was inserted orally and the electricity was then applied bilaterally to the temporal areas of the skull with sufficient amperage to induce a grand mal seizure, all with no sedation. Blood-curdling guttural sounds from the patient's throat could be heard by all in the line, and probably others down the hall as well. The now unconscious patient was moved into a 'recovery' room, as someone called out: "Next!"

During a routine clinical conference, I was once actually able to stay the decision to subject a patient to what I felt was unnecessary ECT. The conference was held in a small auditorium where the staff comprised the 'audience' while clinical leadership and the patient occupied a small stage. As the discussion proceeded toward another mindless prescription for ECT, I impulsively jumped up and asked to speak. With unusual authority, despite my minimal staff status at the time, I quoted a journal article, imagined in the moment, that indicated a patient with this history and/or diagnosis would not benefit from this procedure. It was stunning when my claim was uncritically accepted and the patient was exempted from ECT! While relieved for the patient, it was confounding to realize these senior clinicians were so unsure of what they were doing that they accepted an assertion, without question, from a junior staff member and then quickly moved on to the next case so they could get to lunch in a timely manner.

A rather depressed and hopelessly confused male patient was admitted from a state hospital for the criminally insane, with a diagnosis of schizophrenia. Twenty years earlier he had been charged with "carnally abusing a minor" but a series of recent court decisions[9] had ended legal abuses at state hospitals, resulting in his transfer. (Ironically, that was the very hospital to which my internship facility had sent individuals who were adjudged unable to stand trial, sometimes based on my evaluations.) This patient was assessed as damaged beyond any possibility of ever living a non-institutionalized life. Sadly, had he actually been convicted at the time of the abuse, he might have done just a few years in a conventional prison instead of the dungeon in which he had spent the past 20 years. Certainly that would not have been more inhumane.

This state hospital was little more than a warehouse providing only a minimal, anomic existence for the patients. In their book *The Lives They Left Behind, Suitcases from a State Hospital Attic*, D. Penney and P. Statsny, concluded: "After decades most patients had become so habituated to hospital life that they could not envision learning the skills required to live in a world that had changed drastically since they last lived freely in it."[10]

The well-researched concept of Social Breakdown Syndrome[11] was apparent among patients throughout this state hospital. Best described as deterioration in social abilities, interpersonal relationships and general behavior frequently accompanying organic and functional psychoses (especially the schizophrenias), it is a reaction to the patient's environment rather than an inherent part of the psychotic process. For example, the male patient kept isolated from women no longer makes attempts to be attractive to the opposite sex. A person deprived of purposeful activity, or removed from any meaningful occupation, will have no reason to keep track of time, etc. The Social Breakdown Syndrome can be seen in many settings: mental hospitals, prisons, concentration camps, etc. Aware of this, I made the suggestion that perhaps the female ward could share a common Day Room with the male ward as a means to provide more normal male/female social interaction. Unfortunately my suggestion was invalidated because of a misplaced concern about the potential for sexual acting out by these primarily elderly persons who had been on debilitating anti-psychotic medications for most of their lives.

I came away from my experience at this 'asylum' with a profound recognition of the societal indifference bordering on cruelty to the mentally ill. The grilled hot dog remained the high point of the lives of these state hospital inmates leaving them with nothing to do for the rest of their time but to stare at the beige walls. Under the leadership of its director, this institution was not open to change of any sort. Attempting to treat patients in that environment yielded as much return as a grief counselor might have gotten in a concentration camp.

A little more than a year later I was offered a position in a newly established community based setting designed to prevent the need for such state hospitals, and their abuses. In my letter of resignation to the 'asylum' director, copied to the Commissioner of Mental Hygiene, I attempted to express my disappointment and frustration with the dysfunctionality of the institution and its leadership. The style of my letter is emblematic of the time in which it was written, a time when arbitrary authority had begun to be questioned and confronted in many areas of society. In retrospect, at least in part, it seems I anticipated the modern advances inherent in the community mental health movement I was about to join. Here are some excerpts from this letter:

> My desire to leave is the result of the unpleasant professional atmosphere of this hospital, a factor which is largely a function of both active attempts on your part to maintain the status quo of a hospital still running on nineteenth century concepts of the nature of behavioral disorder, as well as your apparent passive unwillingness to respond to requests for change. . . . I believe you are well acquainted with my attempts over the past year to make constructive, documented, reasonably thought out suggestions for instituting changes in hospital structure and programming which were aimed

at increasing the therapeutic quality of the setting. . . . I made suggestions for the altering of the social structure of the hospital in a
way that would de-emphasize the chain of command concept of the
general medical and surgical hospital, and would create a more democratic atmosphere where lower echelon employees, such as attendants, would feel more a part of the decision making process and
consequently be more effective employees. . . . (I made) suggestions
for specific therapeutic programs for the patients. I initiated, for
example, the painting of murals in back wards in an attempt to make
them more affectively stimulating for the patients. This project was
discontinued after only one trial, due primarily to your unwillingness
to support it. I also attempted to get the more acute patients recently
admitted and housed in a separate building into the back wards so
they could socialize with the chronic patients in an effort to provide
stimulation for the chronic patients and an increased sense of self-
esteem from helping others for the admission patients. This project,
outlined in a memorandum, sat on your desk all summer until it was
finally communicated to me informally that your approval was not
really needed. On the other hand, when I subsequently initiated a
project that provided a professional staff advisor for the attendants
of each of the several back wards, I learned that you were displeased
because your permission was not sought in advance. . . . In the
course of the year and one quarter that I have been in your employ,
the only time I ever talked with you was during the first week when
we were introduced. Since that time I have neither had the opportunity to discuss anything with you although I have made such a
request, nor have you ever formally answered any of my memo-
randa concerning programs. . . . This summer it became increasingly
clear to me that you just don't think non-medical people really have
very much to say concerning the therapeutic program of this hospital . . . the more the non-medical professional has to say about therapeutic planning, the less medical the issue becomes and the status of
the (medical) doctor is threatened, (as noted in *The Myth of Mental
Illness* by Thomas Szasz).[12] . . . I believe the current structure of
this hospital is based on this premise and, therefore, as Belknap has
pointed out in *Human Problems of the State Hospital*,[13] and Dunham and Weinberg in *The Culture of the State Mental Hospital*,[14]
the non-medical professional is rendered relatively useless in terms
of the degree to which he can make full use of his perhaps more
relevant training. . . . To illustrate attempts at artificially based status

in this institution, I might point out that parking, dining and housing facilities are all allocated on the basis of a medical hierarchy concept with (medical) doctors always having first choice. Attendants in this hospital are still taught to stand when a physician and some other professionals enter a room. . . . The books I referred to above, as well as the people here in the hospital, told me when I initiated project planning that I must anticipate and work with resistance to change from the lower echelon employees. While there was some of this, the primary resistance came from representatives of the administration who cited lack of financial resources and lower echelon resistance to change as the basis for *their* lack of endorsement to suggestions. Yet none of my suggestions entailed the spending of any money and, as I have pointed out, lower echelon resistance was not as great as was anticipated and was not a difficult factor to overcome when it was present. It seems to me, therefore, that there is a general lack of a feeling for the general attitudes of the average employee in this hospital on the part of the administration. I believe such statements as, "there is no money," or "Albany has to study it," as was the case in a suggestion to "desegregate" dining facilities, are active ploys used by the administration to continually remind people, like myself, of who really is in charge. I also believe that the administration projects its own inability to accept change onto lower echelon employees and utilizes this factor to rationalize its own inertia.

I never received a response from either the director or the Commissioner of Mental Hygiene. The treatment provided to those chronically mentally ill, predominantly low socio-economic status patients, as I observed it during my internship and state hospital experiences, haunted me then and has continued to inform my work to this day.

Notes

1   D. Barry, No Longer Anonymous: Gravedigger Gets His Due At a Psychiatric Hospital. *The New York Times*, Vol. CLXIV, No. 56, 724, December 23, 2014.
2   Ibid.
3   D. Barry, Restoring Lost Names, Recapturing Lost Dignity. *The New York Times*, Vol. CLXIV, No. 56, 699, November 28, 2014.
4   J. J. Cooper, *Oregon Mental Hospital to Honor 'Forgotten Souls'*, The Associated Press, June 6, 2014.
5   One of the first anti-psychotic medications.

6   Lysergic acid diethylamide – a psychedelic drug known for its potent mood altering effects. Also known as "acid", a person taking this drug is said to be "tripping". Drugfreeworld.org
7   With apologies to William Gladstone, British politician, 1809–1898, who said, "Justice delayed is justice denied." Address to Parliament on the adoption of the disestablishment of the Church of Ireland as a policy of the Liberal Party, on 16 March 1868.
8   A deliberate mischaracterization of the therapy often used in treating personality disorders known as Dialectical Behavior Therapy (DBT).
9   New York Correction History Society website: Brief summary. (The courts eventually ruled that patients transferred there were entitled to a court hearing, the same right as any ordinary citizen involuntarily committed to a civil mental hospital. These abuses included committing persons, even for minor offenses, for 30 to 40 years.)
10   D. Penney, and P. Stastny, *The Lives They Left Behind, Suitcases from a State Hospital Attic*, New York, NY: Bellevue Literary Press, 2008.
11   "Some patients manifest progressive chronic deterioration chiefly by behavior changes which are observable as modifications of personal and social behavior." E. M. Gruenberg, The Social Breakdown Syndrome – Some Origins. *American Journal of Psychiatry*, Vol. 123, No. 12, June 1967.
12   T. Szasz, *The Myth of Mental Illness*, New York, NY: Harper & Row, 1961.
13   I. Belknap, *Human Problems of the State Hospital*, New York, NY: McGraw-Hill, 1956.
14   H. W. Dunham, and S. K. Weinberg, *The Culture of the State Mental Hospital*, Detroit, MI: Wayne State University Press, 1960.

Chapter 4

The Community Mental Health Center

"Give me your tired, your poor"

In 1963 President John F. Kennedy signed into law the Community Mental Health Act[1] providing federal funding for nationwide Community Mental Health Centers. A fundamental objective of this Act was to shut down the appalling state hospital system, with the expectation that the resultant flood of discharged chronically ill patients would be treated in their communities at the newly funded Community Mental Health Centers (CMHCs). Facilitating this process was the concurrent development of new anti-psychotic medications that contributed to the reduction of symptoms in the chronically mentally ill. As well, the findings of several major epidemiological studies of communities such as Chicago,[2] Nova Scotia[3] and midtown New York City[4] demonstrated a clear relationship between social disorganization in communities and the prevalence of mental illness. This was something I had independently noted early in my career: the greater the social disorganization, the greater the prevalence of mental illness.

Now, at last, there was some hope.

"Moral Treatment" as prologue

In the early 1800s, the concept of "Moral Treatment"[5] of mental disorders briefly emerged. It was based on humane psychosocial care and religious and moral discipline. "Moral Treatment" became a relatively widespread treatment approach, as effective or even more effective than much of our current psychiatric practice but, by the mid-1800s, it had fallen into decline due to overcrowding and misuse of asylums as well as a rise in the use of frequently bizarre[6] biomedical 'treatments' such as extended hot and cold baths and spinning chairs suspended from the ceiling. In one sense then, Community Mental Health was somewhat like reinventing the wheel in its focus on the social, individual and occupational needs of patients.

In the 1970s "Moral Treatment" was re-conceptualized in the form of an experiment, known as the Soteria Project,[7] led by Loren Mosher, M.D., Director of the Center for Schizophrenia Studies at the National Institutes of Mental Health. Dr. Mosher was convinced the benefits of medication were overhyped. As in "Moral Treatment", the idea was "to treat people as people, as human beings, with dignity and respect". Essentially the Soteria Project was an attempt at a "solution that could humanize the schizophrenic experience". It "demonstrated that a flexible, community based, non-drug, residential psychosocial program manned by non-professional staff can do as well as a more conventional community mental health program". The initial results at six weeks showed that psychotic symptoms had abated in the Soteria patients to the same degree as in medicated patients. Even more striking, the Soteria patients stayed well for longer periods of time. Relapse rates were lower for the Soteria group at both one-year and two-year follow-ups. The Soteria patients were also functioning better socially – better able to hold jobs and attend school.

Dr. Mosher's impressive findings, however, flew in the face of rigidly held convictions that medication was the primary and preferred (i.e. more economical and profitable) approach to the treatment of schizophrenia. As a result, he and his findings were eventually discredited by the psychiatric establishment despite the numerous studies that called into question the efficacy and safety of the current, widely used psychotropic medications.[8]

The rise of the community mental health movement

In contrast with previous treatment models, community mental health stipulated a wide variety of services: inpatient, outpatient, day hospital, night hospital, crisis intervention, home services, community outreach and prevention for adults, adolescents and children. 'Continuity of care' was mandated, i.e. the same staff would follow patients, in so far as possible, through various clinical stages and treatment services in order to sustain reliable patient information and to preserve established therapeutic alliances and relationships. For the first time, this full range of mental health services would be available. What follows are the areas in which I had direct experience.

Inpatient services

Patients admitted to the inpatient units were those with impaired judgment, compromised reality orientation and a sufficient degree of disorganization to necessitate a safe, controlled environment until it was felt their acute symptoms had abated sufficiently to allow them to be safely moved to less intensive care and management, such as day treatment or the outpatient service. The goal for inpatients was acute symptom reduction and more appropriate, less self-defeating behaviors in order to realize discharge. This would be achieved via various psychotherapies, as well as medication, administered within a therapeutic milieu. Ideally an incentive was created to seek outpatient follow-up, thus improving the odds of avoiding relapse.

Day treatment

People at risk of relapse or in need of ongoing monitoring and feedback in order to sustain their adjustment were candidates for day treatment programs.

The anticipated outcome was maximization of their ability to function in the community. Extensive sustained therapeutic interventions were planned, based on clinical judgment and close monitoring of compliance, optimally on a daily basis. Case management, medication, various forms of individual, group and family psychotherapy, and a variety of activity and recreational groups were central to the clinical approach.

Day treatment proved to be one of the most beneficial options for the management of chronically ill patients. Economically and emotionally it was much less expensive and much less stigmatizing and invasive than confinement on an inpatient unit. Day treatment was the far gentler, more effective option, and was much more likely to lead to long-lasting positive outcomes for the patient.

Outreach services

At the inception of the Community Mental Health Center, outreach to various organizations in the community, including schools, civic groups and religious institutions, was a stipulation of the federal funding grants we received. For example, a social worker and I were assigned to meet with the teachers at a nearby Catholic grade school to determine the mental health services we could offer. Mostly young nuns, these teachers requested ongoing consultation for assistance in dealing with emotional problems detected in their classes. They asked us to help identify which students should be referred for professional treatment and which they might help on their own, with our continued consultation and support.

Not surprisingly, our discussions with the nuns gravitated toward issues relating to the ongoing anti-war protests, as well as the sexual revolution taking place in the late 1960s. Anti-establishment was the zeitgeist,[9] and we recognized the inner turmoil many of the nuns were experiencing over the viability and narrowness of their chosen vocation. In our ongoing meetings, they frequently characterized their life style as constricted and conflicted. Over the next year or two, several left their religious order and re-entered the secular world. Ultimately our dialogue led many of us to question similar rigidities inherent in the mental health system.

Geographic catchment area

In accordance with the hospital's contracts with various funding agencies, when community mental health was first implemented only patients from a certain geographic 'catchment area' were eligible for treatment at the CMHC. The possible use of a false address or other subterfuge to subvert the geographic limits was always of concern and there were even staff members who appointed themselves guardians and enforcers of these restrictions, impervious to the acuity or pain and suffering of the presenting patient.

Staff angst over the possible abuse of our catchment area sovereignty reached the pinnacle of absurdity when a homeless woman who was living in her car sought treatment. Each time she came to the mental health center a serious discussion actually ensued as to whether or not she was eligible based on where she had parked her car that day! In order to contain my own frustration with the staff's rigidity, I sarcastically commented that the woman was obviously 'auto-erratic' and pointed out that alternate side-of-the-street parking days would likely compound the problem.

Community meetings

Morning community meetings were attended by most of the patients and staff, and were an important component of both day treatment and inpatient services. Not only did they help to foster a sense of community and empowerment, they also provided patients with an orientation to date and time, as well as to the daily activity and therapy schedules. Interpersonal contacts and communication were facilitated, social barriers between staff and patients were often reduced, and conflict resolution among the participants was supported. There were opportunities for modeling positive interpersonal relationships through staff/staff and staff/patient interactions. Patients were helped to develop empathy for the needs of others, resulting in a more balanced sense of responsibility. There is substantial objective evidence that regular community meetings such as these significantly reduce violent episodes in institutional settings.[10]

To help set a relaxed, friendly tone, our meetings often started with something humorous. Here are two examples taken from a forgotten book of jokes we used: "People who take cold baths don't have rheumatism, but they do have cold baths!" "My grandmother started walking five miles a day when she was 65. Now she's 90 and we don't know where the hell she is!"

At a memorable community meeting on the inpatient unit, about 40 patients were assembled in their usual circle. The patient-chairperson, under the gentle yet firm control of the staff, conducted the meeting. The patient-secretary read aloud the minutes of the previous meeting. General discussion then ensued and included the usual gripes about food, lack of privileges, allegations of staff abuse, and interpersonal animosities. One of the patients at this particular meeting was a rather short man in his mid-50s who had remained completely silent for the previous 60 days of his hospitalization despite all attempts to get him to speak. He was considerably regressed, to the point that his diet consisted of virtually all stages of the nitrogen cycle. Suddenly, however, in the middle of this meeting he began to show some interest in his surroundings and to mumble, but so softly his words could not be not be understood. Staff and patients alike strained excitedly to hear these first words. Someone called out: "Quiet everyone! Murray is speaking. . . . Speak Murray, speak to us." (Not his real name.) Supportive murmurings came from the group. Sprinklings of, "Speak Murray, speak" could be heard round the circle, staff and patients expressing excitement at the potential revelatory nature of Murray's first words after all this time. A hush descended on the group. Murray, his legs dangling above the floor, raised his round, almost hairless head and, looking at no one in particular said, "Is it okay to jerk off on your knees?" Chaos ensued. "Quiet Murray . . . don't speak," a highly trained staff member was heard to say. Others echoed similar thoughts: "Don't speak . . . don't speak." The meeting ended with everyone feeling confused and unsettled, including Murray who, apparently perplexed by the mixed message he had been given, said no more right up until he was transferred to a long-term state hospital.

Another inpatient community meeting was brought to a complete halt when a patient extemporaneously recited the entire "Rime of the Ancient Mariner", a rather long poem by Samuel Taylor Coleridge. The rapt attention he received belied any idea that hospitalized psychiatric patients are too distractible to participate in meetings of any length.

Clinical staff meetings

Occasionally it was helpful to interject an element of humor into these meetings in order to encourage more spontaneous and thoughtful engagement in discussions. For example, we once had a female patient with malformed facial features who was often mocked by somewhat insensitive staff members. The issue of her work history was being discussed at one treatment planning conference so, taking the staff's insensitivity to its logical conclusion I said (deadpan), "She works as a 'gargoyle' on weekends." The staff members initially nodded in serious acknowledgement until they realized, about ten seconds later, that the point being made was that they were more than eager to accept negative or strange comments about her, no matter how preposterous.

During these meetings a staff member would sometimes voice a moralistic complaint about the rationale for continuing to treat a patient they considered a malingerer. My retort: "He's probably 'faking' that!" After all, would, anyone in their right mind(!) fake their way into intensive psychiatric treatment? Certainly it wouldn't be for the gourmet food. The objection was pejorative and an over-simplification of someone's behavior.

Similarly, complaints were raised as to why we were treating a patient with a history of violence or extensive sociopathic behaviors (another antiquated diagnostic label hiding moralistic attitudes), perhaps child molestation or homicide. "Well, nobody's perfect," I would observe, confronting the professionally inappropriate moralism of this protest. It's one thing for a staff member to object, with rational, seriously thoughtful concerns, to a direction they disagree with regarding treatment of a patient. It is quite another matter when someone states categorically, "I'm not comfortable doing that." My reply, in frustration with such narcissism, was: "Then wear looser clothing!"

Often there were complaints about patients being "uninteresting", even "boring". My reply was, "There are no uninteresting, boring patients, only clinicians who are not listening!"

A culture of inappropriate indifference predominated during some of the early clinical conferences in the day treatment service. At one meeting where a staff member was reading a magazine, I asked the other participants to speak more softly so as not to disrupt her concentration! The magazine immediately disappeared. In a similar disregard of professionalism, a number of women were knitting during the meetings. I asked that this distracting practice promptly cease or I would bring my carpentry project. With their inappropriate behavior now revealed in stark perspective, I had everyone's attention. Professionalism reigned.

Directors' meetings

The weekly meetings of the directors of services in the psychiatry department were generally short on substance but long on posturing and faux problem solving. Occasionally I found it necessary to interject an element of humor in order to sustain intelligent thought. For example, seated at the head of the conference table, the chairman began one meeting by commenting on the growing geriatric problems among certain members of the professional staff referring, in particular, to one "aging" psychologist he alleged was cognitively impaired. "Don't worry," came my spontaneous quip. "In a few years you'll probably forget all about it!"

On a more serious note, however, suddenly and without warning we were confronted with two real problems: The finance officer reported we were currently spending $300,000 a year, an amount of money he apparently considered excessive, on medication for indigent psychiatric outpatients. The director of the inpatient unit then related their beds were being underutilized to which the finance officer tersely responded that this loss of income was compounding the negative effect on our budget. Unstated, perhaps overlooked, was the fact that chronically ill patients were being successfully managed in the day treatment program obviating the need for frequent hospitalization. Apparently that was now being seen as bad for business. A sense of helplessness set in. These were not the kinds of problems our professional training had prepared us to solve. This was business!

Recognizing that the solution would become evident to he who thought like a businessman rather than an ethical clinician, and with an attempt at tension-reducing humor but also subtle sarcasm, I suggested we must immediately discontinue all free medication to indigent outpatients (why aren't they earning a living anyway?) thereby instantly saving $300K. Most of these patients would then quickly decompensate to a level requiring inpatient admission thus filling beds and raising the income of the inpatient unit to the amount required to balance our budget. Problem solved!

As it turned out, my sardonic suggestion wasn't too far from what would soon become reality. As budgets got tighter, the chairman of the department would sometimes call on a Friday to inform me that the inpatient bed census was low. Did I, the director of the day treatment service with a large number of seriously and chronically ill patients, have anyone who might benefit from a long weekend in the hospital? Yes, a number of our patients certainly might have benefited from the amenities of an inpatient stay, but this was ethically and legally a gray area, so while I tried to be supportive and sound cooperative, I never actually complied. The chairman was simply trying to develop what he regarded as humane strategies to maintain the fiscal soundness of the department for the greater good but, as has been said, "Once you give up your integrity, the rest is a piece of cake."[11] My imagined solution had begun to morph into reality.

Ultimately, many more clinical decisions and outcomes would be gauged from an economic perspective. For example, at one meeting a senior executive reported they were seeing a lower than average incidence of respiratory disorders that summer, in children from our area who came to us for treatment. He lamented on the negative impact this was having on our budget. Something that should have been celebrated as medical progress was now bemoaned as a fiscal set-back.

Another example is the patient who likely could have been hospitalized fewer times a year if he could have afforded the newer, more expensive anti-psychotic medications. Since he couldn't, the doctors prescribed the older medications so, here again, it was finances that influenced the clinical decision, not what was best for the patient.

A 2014 *New York Times* article quoted critics of this unscrupulous cost-saving-trend-masquerading-as-medical-decision-making and characterized it as a "form of rationing". The article went on to say, "Some doctors see a potential conflict in trying to be both providers of patient care and financial overseers."[12]

A few months later, the writer of a *New York Times* op-ed piece made the point that low wage workers have neither the resource of Medicaid nor sufficient personal funds to pay for the medications better suited to treat their symptoms, and so they are limited to the less costly ones associated with significantly greater risk for side effects.[13]

The business of health professionals had now become business.

Administration

The administrative side of the mental health system was becoming increasingly burdened not only with major budget concerns, but also with overwhelming regulations and endless documentation requirements. The relentless frustration was becoming emotionally draining and a distraction from the actual clinical work, ostensibly the rationale for the existence of a mental health facility.

My attempt to cope with this kind of stress was exemplified by the memos I regularly sent to our administrator, outlining both the major and minor needs of the unit. At first these memos either went completely unheeded or were met with noncommittal responses. Then I implemented two novel memo forms: The same memo was sent to the administrator for 20 consecutive business days (one calendar month), changing only the date. This was followed by a request for a "subscription renewal". After that, I added a weekly summarizing memo, ranking by importance the top ten concerns of the unit, with a column indicating the number of weeks each had been on the list, similar to what *The New York Times* does with best selling books. Taking this all in good humor, the slightly embarrassed administrator was finally moved to expedite a number of my requests.

An example of administrative absurdity was the initial denial of my request to purchase an optical scanner at a cost of approximately $3,000, not an outrageous expenditure for a hospital with a budget in the millions. A scanner would simplify the process of scoring the objective psychological screening tests administered to all newly admitted patients, and would facilitate an analysis of the data by means of an automated report. "Too expensive", the administrator said.

Not long afterward, I saw an ad offering the scanner at a sale price of $2,500. Sensing an opportunity I brought this 'bargain price' to the attention of this same administrator. "Well certainly," he said. "If it's a bargain, then of course we should buy it!!!" This was a clear example of decision-making based on the arbitrary nature of personal attitudes, a not infrequent occurrence.

Overall, sometimes the farce is with you!

Deconstricting the student experience

Psychology and psychiatry students rotated through all services in our CMHC. In the interest of promoting a non-hierarchical approach to our training programs, I would frequently ask new students how they had gotten this far in their careers. They would look at me quizzically, wondering what I wanted to hear, which was precisely my point. After they had given up trying to find the 'right' answer, I would suggest that probably what they had always done was try to figure out what their supervisors wanted to hear and then respond accordingly. Invariably there would be general, if slightly embarrassed, agreement with my observation after which I would encourage them not to do that here but rather to try to openly express what was actually on their minds and not be intimidated by supervisors or the 'experienced' staff. Experience is often just a matter of making the same mistake over and over again. I then acknowledged that their attempts to be compliant with my suggestion of non-compliance would seemingly be a direct contradiction to the original point and they would, therefore, throughout their tenure here, be immersed in an ongoing struggle with a logical contradiction, the outcome hopefully leading to a greater sense of intellectual independence, a greater tolerance for ambiguity and a resistance to the status quo.

Tradition versus progress

A clearly archaic yet enduring symbol of tradition in the health-care field is the addressing of medical doctors by their title and last name while the rest of the staff are simply addressed by their first names:

"Nancy, get a psychosocial on this patient."
"Yes, Dr. Jones."

This tradition is reminiscent of my experiences at the state hospital where 'non-professionals' were required to stand whenever a 'professional' entered the room. It is, I believe, a disrespectful overstatement of role differences and its perpetuation reinforces hierarchical parent/child-like relationships between doctors and the rest of the staff. Over the years, my many attempts to end this practice within my own work settings have met with minimal success, resistance coming oddly enough from both sides.

There was one brief winning moment when I was chairing a clinical meeting and a very senior psychiatrist entered the room. Addressing me as "*Mr.* Chairman", he sat down and proceeded to join in the discussion. Deadpan, I said, "It's *Dr.* Chairman!"

In 1966 Harold Lasswell and Robert Rubinstein described an experience at Yale Psychiatric Institute[14] based initially on the premise that professional clinical staff laboring under an autocratic, hierarchical tradition would be more effective as professionals if given enhanced clinical independence and greater input into decision-making. They focused on historically inflexible styles of leadership that continued to preclude clinical opportunities for more progressive and democratically arrived at policy decision-making.

Early in the development of the CMHC, this approach was reflected in the democratic model of 'empowerment' seemingly espoused by leadership. Nevertheless, there occurred a very significant example of the persistence of traditional organizational inertia despite the new progressive rhetoric being advanced. In a break from traditional nursing practices and expectations, three nurses were hired exclusively for the day shift with the intent of broadening their therapeutic roles. This was a major change as virtually all nurses at the time were required to rotate periodically to other shifts, but it was in sync with other progressive moves being made by the organization. Shortly thereafter, however, these nurses were told by their supervisor that some unforeseen scheduling problem required that they accept periodic rotation to the night shift on the inpatient unit. Recognizing this as a betrayal and violation of their hiring agreement, the three nurses refused this re-reassignment and were then fired. Although most of the staff vigorously protested the decision to let the nurses go, management remained bound by stereotypic, traditional expectations of nursing roles. The staff was left feeling deceived and thus skeptical about the possibility for successful participatory democratic decision-making opportunities, and became less receptive to open dialogue and planning. This incident, among others, undermined the democratically oriented model advocated by Lasswell and Rubenstein and, ostensibly, by our own leadership.

The problem was further compounded by those who had historically been delegated authority for clinical and policy decisions. Psychiatrists and unit leaders realized they could be held individually accountable for democratically arrived at decisions. As well, the attendant threat to their traditionally preeminent status led to their resistance to any reduction in their authority, further limiting any semblance of collective decision-making.

In reaction to this ambiguity, the staff eventually split into factions: pro-professionalism versus anti-professionalism, hierarchical versus consensual/democratic decision-making, those for more independent responsibility versus those against it. It soon became obvious that this divide, perhaps better characterized as ambivalence in the face of change, resulted from the mixed messages coming from the leadership of the CMHC. A long struggle ensued resulting ultimately in most authority remaining, as it had always been, in the hands of the few. Many of us were quite discouraged by this outcome but, despite all the sturm und drang,[15] limited consensus-oriented policy and clinical decision-making persisted.

Doing the right thing

In the early days of community mental health and day treatment, we were all caught up in an 'anything goes' ethos. Home visits were one of our new and flashy approaches to treatment; no matter where the patient was at the time of an acute episode, we went. Three examples:

A small, gaunt female patient on our day treatment service was known to become acutely psychotic from time to time, often for reasons we couldn't explain, but sometimes as a toxic reaction to inappropriately high dosages of prescribed medication. On occasion her psychiatrist could perform 'miraculous cures' simply by reducing her dose! One evening the patient's daughter called us to say her mother had become severely disoriented and disorganized. Could we help? We sure could! A psychiatrist, a nurse and I drove over to her apartment in the doctor's car and quickly determined she needed to be hospitalized. We literally picked up this tiny woman and, with minimal resistance, took her to the emergency department for admission. Need I add that she improved considerably when her medication was reduced? Of course, in today's litigious atmosphere we could never do that. Instead we would call the police and an ambulance and persuade them the patient needed to be taken to the emergency department for evaluation and hospitalization. In those days, however, we were above and beyond such legal niceties. We did what was 'right'!

On another day, one of our patients called the hospital saying he had swallowed all his anti-psychotic medication and was now drinking a lot of beer; his stated intention was to die. At first he refused to tell us where he was but eventually gave his address at a bar. We immediately called the police to pick him up and take him to the emergency department. Twenty minutes later, however, the patient called back; his speech was now slurred, but we understood that he had managed to hide when he saw the police entering the bar. I told him to wait right where he was and that I was coming for him.

On that snowy, slushy night I sped to the bar in my own car, relishing the impunity I felt going through red lights on this mission of mercy. (Where are the police when you have a great excuse?) Approaching the bar, I saw the patient stumbling along the street, finally collapsing in a doorway. Had I not actually seen this last movement it is doubtful I would have found him in time. I jumped out of my little sports car, one not designed with ambulance missions in mind, ran over to the doorway, grabbed him under the arms and struggled to get him into the passenger seat. Noting he was rapidly losing consciousness, speeding became essential if I was to get him to the emergency department in time, all the while again hoping to be intercepted by the police either for assistance or to gain an official free pass to violate traffic regulations.

Arriving at the emergency department, I explained the urgent nature of my mission to the triage nurse and kept moving toward an empty stretcher I spotted in the hall. Quickly I cataloged the clinical facts to the staff as they helped me put the now unconscious patient onto the gurney. As we removed his street clothes, a knife with a four-inch blade fell out of his sock.

The patient survived that suicide attempt and eventually returned to out-patient treatment but, sadly, he was left with short-term memory loss and other symptoms consistent with long-term chronic drug and alcohol abuse, as well as the residual effects of the overdose.

At the end of yet another day in the mental health business, one of our mental health workers suddenly appeared and insisted I had to accompany him in the hospital station wagon to rescue a distraught, suicidal patient. It seems she had called to say she intended to kill herself by drinking all her liquid anti-psychotic medication. Although it was not clear at the time whether this medication was lethal, or even if she had a sufficient amount on hand to do herself in, her intent was clear and intervention was indicated.

We contacted the police and they traced the call to a pay phone in front of an ice cream stand at a nearby intersection. Since no one was else available at the time, the mental health worker and I decided to race to the scene ourselves. He drove, speeding through red lights with the delight of someone who has waited all his life for this opportunity. But, since it was the patient who wanted to die and I had already gotten the need for this kind of excitement out of my system in a similar situation, I maturely urged him to slow down and not enjoy himself quite so much.

When we arrived at the intersection, there was our patient, still talking on the pay phone, still drinking from a small medicine bottle. Several people were standing around eating ice cream. As we approached, we saw three surly-looking men begin to surround the patient. The mental health worker prepared to confront them but then we noticed a gun in one man's waistband and a badge hanging from a chain around his neck. They were undercover cops sent to the scene when the call was originally traced. We exchanged identification and then, since they were an anti-crime unit traveling in an undercover taxi with other business to take care of, we mutually agreed we could manage to take this small, unthreatening woman back to the hospital in our station wagon and they could get on with whatever they were doing. (Clearly this was something that today would only be done by Emergency Medical Services.) Several ice cream-eating people of various ages watched with amazing indifference, as five scruffy-looking men picked up that seemingly defenseless woman, tossed her and the bag of groceries at her side into a station wagon and drove away. No one protested, raised a question or attempted to interfere in any way.

It was only a matter of minutes before we reached the emergency department where the patient was formally evaluated and admission to the psychiatric inpatient unit was arranged. Before we left, however, I offered the patient her bag of groceries. "What groceries?" she asked. "Those aren't mine!" We realized then that the colossal indifference of New Yorkers extended as well to their groceries.

Often there were patients who appreciated our 'heroic' efforts to administer care and treatments. One was a somewhat overweight, 40-something female hospitalized on an unlocked ward, in keeping with the progressive attitudes of the new community mental health movement. One day we needed to restrain her to administer an intramuscular (IM) dose of anti-psychotic medication. As we prepared to do so, she suddenly bolted past the door monitor and managed to run down four flights of stairs, out the back door and into the adjacent parking lot, a nurse and I following in hot pursuit. Despite the fact that we had no legal authority outside the hospital building, we overtook the patient half way across the parking lot, gently lowered her to the ground and right there, with several incredulous people watching us, we administered the injection. We then escorted our tired and breathless patient back to the unit where she expressed her appreciation that we had cared enough to charge after her.

The fall of community mental health

Looking back, I recognize how fortunate I was to have emerged from the '19th century', with the archaic attitudes, policies and procedures I witnessed during my training, to join the staff of a CMHC. It was an exciting time with much opportunity for debate, innovation and the 'luxury' to actually treat patients. Regulations? Documentation? Not much then. The concept of community mental health seemed a quantum leap forward in progressive psychiatric treatment yet ultimately this 'new' social policy failed, primarily because of inadequate implementation.[16]

Since there was little federal oversight of the funding in the 1960s and early 1970s, only a handful of the CMHCs actually delivered on their mission while the rest diverted the money to other purposes or, at best, set up traditional outpatient clinics. After much finger pointing and political infighting among the mental health professionals and legislators initially involved in the execution of this approach, the original eight-year staffing grants were not renewed by Congress[17] thus virtually ending this comprehensive approach to the care of individuals with mental health problems. At the very least, it was shortsighted and certainly exposed the minimal political support and inadequate funding for mental health care and thus policy.

Reimagining community mental health

In 2015 a group of "appalled" university based ethicists criticized the inability of our overburdened mental health system to sustain adequate treatment for the mentally ill. They noted: "Deinstitutionalization has really been trans-institutionalization," with prisons now the default and largest of mental health facilities. In suggesting a return to the state mental hospital or "asylum" system, they expected the new "asylums" would be sufficiently funded to absorb the large number of patients in need of sustained care and would provide them with appropriate residential and treatment programs.[18] History, however, suggests the high likelihood that such institutions would eventually revert to the original rigidities and inertia. In their book *The Willowbrook Wars*, the authors noted that with such asylums "there are no eyes on, no one outside is watching, and that becomes an invitation to abuse".[19] Given that social priorities are currently not weighted in favor of health care, there is, of course, no basis for assuming any increase in the funding necessary to support such an endeavor. Perhaps money would be better spent upgrading current community-based inpatient and outpatient treatment and prevention programs. This discussion is interesting but, nevertheless, the immoral, inhumane and shortsighted status quo remains.

An article in *The New York Times* in March 2015 addressed the current excessive use and over-reliance on psychiatric drugs, particularly in nursing homes. As a result of "inadequate numbers of employees" it is now the only means to control patients with dementia, *The Times* concluded.[20]

A study funded by the National Institutes of Mental Health and reported in *The New York Times* in October 2015 concluded that "schizophrenia patients who received smaller doses of antipsychotic medication and a bigger emphasis on one-on-one talk therapy and family support made greater strides in recovery over the first two years of treatment than patients who got the usual drug focused care".[21] Wait! Wasn't that day treatment? Wasn't that the Soteria Project?

An even more recent *New York Times* article (February 2016) reported: "A new approach to treating early schizophrenia, which includes family counseling" as well as help with jobs and schooling, "results in improvements in quality of life that make it worth the added expense".[22] Somewhat reminiscent of the original community mental health grants, isn't it?

And they call this progress!

Notes

1 J. F. Kennedy, *The Community Mental Health Act (also known as the Mental Retardation and Community Mental Health Centers Construction Act of 1963)*, January 31, 1963.
2 R. E. L. Farris, and H. W. Dunham, *Mental Disorders in Urban Areas: An Ecological Study of Schizophrenia and Other Psychoses*, Chicago, IL: University of Chicago Press, 1939.
3 A. H. Leighton, *My Name Is Legion*, New York, NY: Basic Books, 1959.
4 Srole, et al., *Mental Health in the Metropolis. The Midtown Manhattan Study*, New York, NY: McGraw-Hill, 1962.
5 J. S. Bockoven, *Moral Treatment in American Psychiatry*, New York, NY: Springer Publishing, 1972.
6 R. Whitaker, *Mad in America, Bad Science, Bad Medicine, and the Enduring Mistreatment of the Mentally Ill*, New York, NY: Basic Books, 2009.
7 In Greek mythology, Soteria was the goddess or spirit of safety and salvation, deliverance and preservation from harm. Wikipedia.
8 R. Whitaker, *Mad in America, Bad Science, Bad Medicine, and the Enduring Mistreatment of the Mentally Ill*, New York, NY: Basic Books, 2009.
9 "The Zeitgeist (spirit of the age or spirit of the time) is the intellectual fashion or dominant school of thought that typifies and influences the culture of a particular period in time." E. Saarinen, *Shaping the Future*, New Haven, CT: Yale University Press, 2006. p. 15.
10 M. Lanza, J. Rierdan, and L. Forester, Reducing Violence Against Nurses: The Violence Prevention Community Meeting. *Issues in Mental Health Nursing*, Vol. 30, 745–750, 2009.
11 J. R. Ewing, Jr., a fictional character in the hit US television series *Dallas*, aired on CBS (1978–1991).
12 A. Pollack, Treatment Cost Could Influence Doctors' Advice. *The New York Times*, Vol. CLXIII, No. 56, 475, April 18, 2014.
13 E. Larkin, and I. Hurford, Perpetuating Schizophrenia's Stigma. *The New York Times*, Vol. CLXIII, No. 56, 592, August 13, 2014.
14 H. D. Lasswell, and R. Rubinstein, *The Sharing of Power in a Psychiatric Hospital*, New Haven, CT: Yale University Press, 1966.
15 Literally "storm and drive", though usually translated as "storm and stress". Wikipedia.
16 E. F. Torrey, *American Psychosis: How the Federal Government Destroyed the Mental Illness Treatment System*, New York, NY: Oxford University Press, 2014.
17 Ibid.

18 D. A. Sisti, A. G. Segal, and E. J. Emanuel, Improving Long-term Psychi-
    atric Care: Bring Back the Asylum. *JAMA*, Vol. 313, No. 3, 243–244, 2015.
    doi:10.100/jama 2014.16088
19 D. J. Rothman, and S. Rothman, *The Willowbrook Wars: Bringing the Men-
    tally Disabled into the Community*, New York, NY: Routledge, 2017.
20 R. Pear, Psychiatric Drug Overuse Is Cited by Federal Study. *The New York
    Times*, Vol. CLXIV, No. 56, 793, March 2, 2015.
21 B. Carey, New Approach May Alleviate Schizophrenia. *The New York Times*,
    Vol. CLXV, No. 57, 25, October 20, 2015.
22 B. Carey, Study Backs Added Costs for Treating Schizophrenia. *The New
    York Times*, Vol. CLXV, No. 57, 129, February 1, 2016.

Part II

Challenging clinical circumstances

Chapter 5

Compromised patient care

The in-hospitable hospital

Perhaps not surprising, many factors can support or thwart clinicians in their clinical approach to patient care. On some psychiatric units substantial impediments to humane treatment can be observed, many blatantly absurd. In one institution, like a time warp, the setting is reminiscent of my internship: morning rounds involving the entire unit staff, often ten or more at a time, alternately socializing amongst themselves in the halls or entering a patient's room where each patient, usually still in bed, is asked how they are doing. When the patient begins to answer, a staff member invariably interrupts with, "We'll talk about that later. We have to move on now."

As mentioned previously, throughout my internship and state hospital 'adventures' the locked wards, with their massive doors, were accessible only with keys too large and too heavy to fit in a pocket; best to carry them stuck in one's belt, like a weapon. Several years later I worked in a hospital where access to the inpatient unit from the elevator was through a locked, sliding gate creating a truly 'gated' community. The key to this gate was of normal size, perhaps reflecting some progress, however, all the doors on that unit, including the nurses' station, the clerical office, the staff bathroom, the dining room and the activity therapy rooms were locked, all the time, creating a prison like ambience and necessitating the carrying of many of these 'more advanced' keys. Not unlike prison guards, staff were constantly unlocking doors, walking through them and then making sure they were locked behind them.

At this same hospital an administrator, someone with no formal responsibility for the inpatient unit, once had all books, pens and pencils removed because he deemed them a danger to patients and staff. He did this arbitrarily and summarily, without benefit of consultation with the clinical staff and without prior notice to the department leadership, never mind the patients, many of whom reacted strongly to this disempowering and disrespectful action. (This act certainly gave new meaning to term 'throwing the book at you', even though no one could recall a book ever having been thrown.) An unclear protocol was issued a short time later delineating how patients would be permitted to access one book at a time, as well as some limited writing materials.

The staff took the whole thing cynically, one person joking that perhaps only soft covered books should be allowed on the unit only to discover that was indeed the policy. So jokes become policy . . . or was it the other way around? What is the ballistic differential between being hit by a very thick soft covered book and a very thin hard covered book, especially when it never happens?

Repeatedly throughout my entire career I have often heard staff members say that psychiatric patients admitted to the hospital today are sicker than ever before. Given my extensive years in the field, if there were any truth to this, by now patients would be beyond sick, acting out in some alternate universe. One can only speculate this perception was born of the chronic frustration experienced by staff working with poorly conceptualized or understood behavioral disorders, often without the support of competent, vision-oriented leadership, under the progressive and crushing pressure of increasing regulations and the monetary emphasis over clinical and human needs, and all while trying to cope with their own feelings of inadequacy. An all too frequent result is the insensitive, discourteous and abusive treatment of patients.

After assuming the directorship of an inpatient unit in the 1970s, I was confronted with a long-standing arbitrary rule apparently invented by the staff: Once patients were discharged from the unit, they would not be permitted back to visit their inpatient friends. The staff based this rule on the reflexive assumption these patients might become disruptive. Seeing this as both stigmatization and possibly a violation of civil rights, I ordered the practice stopped and limited the prohibition to those who were truly disruptive or anti-social in some destructive way. The rule, however, had a life of its own and occasionally I made unannounced visits to the evening shift to monitor compliance. Obviously, however, I could never be sure of compliance in my absence, and that rule never really died. When my tenure ended, undoubtedly it was resurrected.

Staff insensitivity, to boundaries and patient privacy, as well as slavish adherence to rigid hospital schedules, continues to be pervasive. I have witnessed patients being yanked out of various therapy groups, often in mid-sentence and mid-emotion, for such reasons as the routine administration of medication, taking vital signs, drawing blood, completing paper work and the like. Sometimes a staff member interrupts the dynamic of a group simply to fetch something from a closet in the room. Certainly none of these things was so urgent they could not wait for the group to conclude.

Then there was the autumn evening when several inpatients were watching the last game of the World Series, happily and quietly reveling in the exquisite tension of the game. It was the bottom of the 9th, 2 outs and the winning run on third base when a nurse suddenly appeared, announced it was time for bed and abruptly turned the television off. Outrageous? Certainly, but controlling behavior such as this, completely lacking in anything resembling empathy, compassion, humanity or common sense is not infrequent on inpatient units.

In another institution, just prior to clinical meetings, I observed staff members covering their plastic, non-absorbent chairs with newspaper because patients had recently sat on them. The obvious implication was that the patients had contaminated the chairs. Cynically mentioning to these fastidious 'touch no evil' professionals that one could see unreadable headlines or worse, printed in reverse 'covering their asses' (in more ways than one), resulted in embarrassed shrugs. The procedure became more sophisticated when *The New York Times'* Science Section was used with greater frequency. Perhaps this developing intellectual trend will continue with staff ultimately tearing pages out of *Ulysses*[1] to sit on.

Announcements are frequently heard from the overhead loudspeaker system in most hospitals, the majority unrelated to the business of the psychiatric unit. Not only are they disruptive to meetings and group therapy sessions, but they are often made by staff with shrill voices. Out of sheer frustration I often ask patients if they hear these 'voices' or if it's just me. There is always a supportive laugh in response, but patients who chronically experience auditory hallucinations, even while on medication, acknowledge they often confuse the announcements with their own 'voices' and are distressed by the experience, despairing of the treatability of their symptoms.

As well as announcements, a somewhat garbled version of the song "Turn! Turn! Turn"[2] was recently heard coming through these overhead speakers. You might think this was an attempt at inspirational music for the benefit of psychiatric patients, but it 'turns' out it was a stratagem developed by some expensive redesign committee to remind the staff on medical units to turn comatose or paralyzed patients at regular intervals to avoid bed sores

Perhaps this idea could be expanded to cover additional instructions to staff, thus brightening everyone's mood throughout the day, possibly even eliminating the need for meetings. For instance, "Someone's in the Kitchen with Dinah . . ."[3] could be used to remind patients to come for meals. Or maybe, "Cold Hearted Man"[4] could summon the code team for a cardiac arrest. Or "Ring of Fire"[5] might be a little less unsettling than the usual flashing lights and siren.

Then there is the overhead announcement of "Code Grey" signifying a psychiatric emergency (usually a patient out of control), and routinely involving the hospital security. Can anyone realistically be expected to react effectively in response to such a bland color? Once again, this might be where a musical option would be more useful: "Touch of Grey",[6] for instance, might be a far better mobilizer. Obviously, a course in music appreciation would have to be added to the orientation for new staff. Endless possibilities. Maybe they really are on to something!

Psychiatric patients often complain there is little to do to during the day yet it is well known that even when recreational activities are offered, the patients remain unmotivated or indifferent to these opportunities. Perhaps what is needed on the units is a 'licensed clinical tummler' (LCT).* Using humor, spontaneous social contact and warm engaging rapport development, the LCT's primary, and perhaps only, purpose would be to cajole patients into better moods and then motivate them to participate in available activities. While this may seem whimsical, it might actually turn out to have practical clinical value and perhaps should be pursued as an antidote to the boredom experienced by many inpatients. After all, if we are going to 'turn' the hospital into a musical, then this intervention would be a natural extension of entertainment as clinical practice.

A striking example of less enlightened but expedient (at least in the short run) treatment was revealed by a hospital review of incidents where inpatients had behaved in disorganized or menacing ways requiring staff intervention. The analysis found that approximately eight out of ten of these occurrences resulted in the almost immediate intramuscular (IM) injection of a rapid-acting, mind-numbing anti-psychotic medication. Little consideration was apparently given to attempting less invasive, relationship-based psychotherapeutic interventions prior to administering these injections. Medications were given almost reflexively, with little forethought, since injections required the least amount of effort or clinical skill and were, therefore, the quickest way to handle the

---

* Yiddish for a person who makes things happen, in particular a professional entertainer or comedian whose function is to encourage an audience, guests at a resort, etc., to participate in the entertainment or activities.

situation. Developing a connection with a patient on the spot, and talking them down in a related and even-tempered manner, requires too much time and effort and besides, who's in control here anyway? Essentially the staff point of view is: "I don't think, therefore IM!"[7]

This quick and easy approach can also be found in outpatient clinics where medications are maximally utilized and psychotherapy is reduced to bare bones, perfunctory emotional support rendered in the shortest amount of time possible. This is the result of diminished public funding, staffing cut-backs, the escalation of complex and restrictive governmental regulations, and the demand for more and more documentation. The relentless pressure from profit-driven insurance companies has led to decreasing reimbursement rates and/or the number of allowable treatment sessions.

And then there was the infamous Christmas tree incident. As the holidays approached one year, the inpatient activity staff put up an artificial tree in their area and decorated it with, among other things, tinsel garlands. Along came a senior administrator who decided the tree and the garlands were a danger to patients. Once again, this was someone who had no formal association with this particular unit. Although a dispute ensued with the staff, the administrator was successful in 'protecting' the patients from this 'poisoned tree'. When he had it temporarily placed in the Seclusion Room, I sardonically recommended the tree also be put into four point restraints.[8] Now *that's* ridiculous someone else said.

A group psychotherapy session was about to begin. As several inpatients were voluntarily entering the room, a nurse was heard telling a patient that she could not attend. This was a patient with a history of being a "trouble maker" and had, once again, engaged in some sort of disruptive behavior. When I pointed out to the nurse that group psychotherapy was part of her treatment, she said that she was under strict orders from the psychiatrist to withhold the patient's 'privileges'. Puzzled about treatment being a 'privilege' I left the room for a moment and sought out the psychiatrist who, it turns out, was only implementing the order of another psychiatrist. I asked if the plan was also to withhold the 'privilege' of medication. To her credit, the doctor immediately recognized the contradiction and agreed to allow the patient to participate in the group.

Later, in a clinical staff meeting, this psychiatrist reported on the incident. Using the contradiction I had brought to her attention, she pointed out the distinction between treatment and privileges, and encouraged more rational, less moralistic treatment planning. Hopefully, a more progressive standard was set for the staff going forward.

Win! Win!

A man in his 40s arrived somewhat late to a different inpatient psychotherapy group. Wearing a pained expression he hesitantly told us he had a hernia, and described how he felt pain every time he stood up and had to push 'it' back in. We asked if he had reported this to his medical providers and he said he had, but was told that surgery was not available to psychiatric inpatients and, furthermore, they had no means by which to obtain an interim support device for him. With undisguised sarcasm, someone in the group said: "I guess if this was a real hospital they could actually treat his problem!"

The patient received much support and sympathy from the group and was urged to again approach his medical providers. He said he would try but had little hope of a different response from the people who had already failed to demonstrate any interest in referring him for medical follow-up.

Later that same day, I approached his doctors and asked why no one had taken the patient's complaint seriously. One of them defensively said, "It wasn't that urgent." Somewhat bewildered by the insensitivity displayed here, I responded: "Well, why don't you tell him that? He reports that he is experiencing considerable pain and I'd appreciate your taking another look at him. And, by the way, as required, I have documented his concerns in the group psychotherapy note." Apparently, now that there was a record of their initial indifference, combined with what I would like to believe was some respect for my senior (although not supervisory) status on the staff, the next day all things suddenly became possible: The patient was seen by a surgeon, and an interim support device was soon given to the patient.

This incident illustrates problems with not only staff attitudes but systemic impediments as well, often resulting in the under- or non-treatment of medical problems in psychiatric patients. Chronic short staffing on many inpatient units results in poorly supported, over-worked, disengaged staff who are often required to triage their workloads because they just cannot get to everyone, despite their best efforts. Compounding this is the view of many health professionals that psychiatric patients frequently feign or exaggerate complaints of discomfort or pain related to physical/medical problems. Their view may be any or all of the following: The patient is somaticizing, is malingering, is manipulative, is delusional, it's hysteria, or it's all in his head!

During another inpatient group psychotherapy session a homeless woman told of being sent by taxi to a facility a great distance from here to be interviewed for residential placement. Somehow she was allowed to leave a locked unit by herself, despite hospital policy that required inpatients to always be accompanied by a staff member when leaving the hospital. In fact, the hospital did not permit inpatients out of the building, even for a breath of fresh air. As if the hospital's error wasn't bad enough, once at the other facility the patient was denied the interview because of that agency's rigidly enforced rule requiring the presence of a staff member from the referring hospital before an interview would be conducted. Needless to say, the group members were incredulous.

The patient reported difficulty finding her way back on her own, and when asked why she had even bothered to come back, she replied that all her possessions were here and she really had nowhere else to go.

Later I spoke with the supervising psychiatrist to whom the patient had reportedly addressed her distress about the waste of time and effort that this event had been for her. When I added my own concern about this seemingly irregular circumstance, the psychiatrist's first response was that the patient was a "liar", but then she defensively added that the unit chief had approved it.

Her voice rising with personalized anger (read countertransference), the psychiatrist then described the patient, as a "germaphobe" which she characterized as more of an irritating, narcissistic affectation than a serious psychiatric symptom. She suggested I should cure the patient of this before any further questioning of the incident.

The psychiatrist went on to state the patient was making housing placement more difficult because she wanted her "own studio apartment" with her "own bathroom". Obviously because this was a mental patient with a low socio-economic status, the psychiatrist felt her demands were inappropriate.

When I indicated that I would, of course, include the patient's account in my note for the day so the treating staff would become aware of the patient's concerns, the psychiatrist warily 'suggested' she didn't think this was a good idea and I should just put some "general stuff" in the note (read that as 'don't make trouble'). I replied that since the unit chief approved this, what exactly was her concern? She had no immediate answer and then seemed to withdraw from the discussion. I entered my note as planned.

This incident exemplifies the kind of personalized, defensive, condescending, moral judgment that masquerades as objective psychiatric opinion, as well as a trivialization of the work I do.

A 'touching' moment

The following story illustrates another needless and preventable mishandling of a sensitive situation on the part of poorly led staff, and suggests that management was ultimately responsible for this failure.

An edgy, chronically hostile inpatient became upset and agitated one morning, for reasons unknown. In an attempt to soothe and calm him, a female patient sitting next to him leaned over and gently patted his leg. While this was a seemingly innocent and supportive act, a female staff member witnessing it angrily demanded that the touching stop at once and that the 'offending' female leave the area.

In group psychotherapy later that day this was the first topic of the session. The male patient's account was confirmed by the 'toucher', i.e. the female patient. The involved staff member was also a participant in the group and she became increasingly angry and defensive as the event was discussed. "That's the rule," she repeated, loudly and indignantly, and it became necessary to try to calm her down. Eventually she moved back and sat apart from the group. Clearly personal problems were interfering with her professional judgment. The two patients involved, as well as several others, were visibly upset.

In an attempt to diffuse the situation I pointed out that while the rule exists as perhaps the only solution to avoid potentially harmful and inappropriate behavior, touching is clearly an acceptable human behavior and not at all deviant. Ideally, as professionals we aim to provide inpatients with a more 'normal' experience than they might have previously been a part of, however, the prohibition against touching is admittedly at variance with that goal, thus creating a contradiction for the people involved. Unfortunately that contradiction contributed to the conflict today but certainly we can try to find a way to set clear limits without demeaning or demonizing the protagonists. It is very important for staff to be sensitive, professional and objective in these kinds of situations.

Ultimately the discussion had a calming and validating effect on the entire group, especially the original participants.

Mal-practice

An example of what might be called 'Residential Disposition Dysfunction' (RDD) involved a male patient in his mid-30s, living a desperately lonely life. A number of arbitrary stumbling blocks had hindered outpatient placement thus he had remained on the inpatient unit for several months. Although he wanted to enter an adult group home, he was stymied because the home did not accept his insurance and, even more striking, his history of drug abuse and suicidal behaviors had resulted in repeated rejections from similar facilities. The inpatient staff had concluded he was 'resistant' and thus held him responsible for his situation. (Who's resistant?) We were confronted with the paradox of private, profit-oriented adult homes, once hailed as more humane alternatives to state hospitals, accepting only the most manageable patients in order to minimize their expenses and responsibilities while maximizing their profits. There's no place like (an adult) home.

A highly intelligent inpatient in his 50s had grown up under abusive conditions and had never known a stable living environment. He was a chronic drug abuser with little work experience. His psychiatric history included multiple stays on our inpatient unit from which he was generally resistant to discharge. A few months prior to this present admission, he had attempted suicide in the bathroom of another psychiatric hospital; he told me he had paused in that attempt because he was able to imagine me telling him not to do it. He also told me the staff at that hospital had warned him not to make such 'gestures' on their unit as it created a lot of paper work for them, which he interpreted as a hint he should wait until leaving the hospital. His 'gesture', he said, was precipitated by what he perceived as the staff's indifference to him, not difficult to believe based on his descriptions. Essentially, it was his recollection of where the system had worked for him, and where he had developed a treatment alliance with someone who cared that saved his life.

His current discharge-resistance was based on his clear understanding that he would be relegated to a single room occupancy facility (SRO) in a neighborhood he didn't know, to live an anomic life. He complained that his caseworker knew less than he did about how to go about getting him a better placement and he was right about that.

I suggested he might give new meaning to his life by using his experiences to help others by becoming a peer counselor, and that he attend weekly individual psychotherapy. These ideas, for the first time, gave him a realistic and revivifying goal, one he embraced with enthusiasm, but the staff failed to follow up on these recommendations and so he clung to his life on the inpatient unit, despite its drawbacks, because it gave him a community, structure and comfort unknown anywhere else.

As the staff grew more and more frustrated with him, clinical objectivity morphed into moralism. While participating in the routine, mindless rounds one morning, I tried to get the staff to understand that his resistance was essentially based on his very human (read non-pathological) fear of loneliness and lack of structure. They felt he was manipulative and malingering ("he was probably faking that"), and had essentially "brought it all upon himself". These were their conflated moral and clinical observations when in actuality the patient was simply trying to survive in a system offering very limited support.

Ultimately he was discharged to an SRO and a chemical dependency program, but a month or so later he turned up in the emergency department at another hospital requesting transfer back to our unit. When the staff learned of this, there was muttering that he was just a self-absorbed "pain in the ass" who sponged off others and, somehow, his request was effectively blocked. So much for non-judgmental treatment of the mentally ill in the 21st century!

A very bright, articulate, unemployed émigré had been living in this country for a number of years. In addition to severe depression and suicidal thoughts, his presenting complaints on admission to the inpatient unit included gangrene in his leg that he feared would become contagious to others. (It turned out he did not have gangrene, and anyway it's not generally thought to be contagious.)

Several years earlier he had lost his high paying technology job and, over time, his skills had become increasingly irrelevant. To the exclusion of all other activities, he had been taking care of his elderly mother who had recently fallen, broken her hip and was now close to death in a nursing facility. He blamed himself for her accident and feared irrevocable social isolation without her. Reasoning that since we are all going to die eventually, and given the futility of life, it would make sense to end his life sooner rather than later. He was concerned, however, that any attempt he made on his own life might endanger others as well, an ambivalent expression of suicidal ideation if ever there was one.

The staff initially dismissed him as self-centered, someone with a "personality disorder" who simply craved attention. There was, however, the possibility they were oversimplifying and distorting a more complex problem as a function of their very own human anxieties about mortality. Many of the staff had apparently never confronted the threatening idea of the inevitably of death so articulately stated by this patient.

When we talked about this in a group psychotherapy session, the patients became visibly anxious as they listened to him speak, and urgently tried to talk him 'into life'. I suggested to the group that perhaps he had a point and maybe we should consider his idea, not just dismiss it out of hand. As a result of the discussion, by the end of the session the patients had arrived at much more life-affirming conclusions, recognizing that an awareness of one's limited mortality might encourage and support making the most of our lives.

Individual psychotherapy for this patient centered on a number of related issues. He was able to acknowledge that his social isolation was connected to his enmeshment in his mother's life and agreed that the specter of her declining health was even more difficult and painful than what he anticipated he would experience after her death. He also came to realize he had always harbored very grandiose expectations for personal achievement and when they hadn't been realized, he concluded life did not seem worth continuing. When presented with the idea that maybe he could compromise by achieving an 'interesting' life, in contrast to a great and brilliant one, he became somewhat intrigued and agreed to consider this alternative. He genuinely enjoyed our verbal interactions, particularly about humor and music, especially Mozart, so I suggested this might be a model for how to enjoy and value life. He had made several friends on the unit and perhaps this could give life some meaning after all.

Another unsettling aspect of this case involved the patient's request for replacement reading glasses since he had left his at home when he was admitted. The staff told him they could do nothing about that, it was not their policy (even though there was an eye clinic in the hospital). In their professional opinion, if he couldn't get new glasses in the hospital, it would be further motivation for him to get sufficiently better in order to be discharged so he could return home to where he had left his glasses.

The bureaucratic inflexibility, and the assumption this demonstrates that the patient could will himself to be better with such an incentive, underlines once again the rigid, judgmental and even ignorant attitudes frequently found in the health-care system. On the positive side, however, the patient was helped to recognize that his request for glasses was further evidence of his renewed interest in living. He accepted a plan requiring his commitment to 'life' and subsequent discharge to a day program that could replicate the community of patients he found here.

Overall, despite his view that the treating staff was excessively controlling, and indifferent and disrespectful of his privacy, the patient actually received better care than most, in part because he was such an intelligent, likeable man. His treatment reversed the downward emotional spiral that previously had made death seem like a welcome escape and, it might be argued, the bureaucratic frustrations that provoked anger in him allowed for ventilation of his depression and ultimately proved to be therapeutic.

A very anxious inpatient who rarely spoke shared a room with another patient diagnosed as 'selectively' mute but, in fact, never spoke at all. When I suggested this was not a beneficial combination and one of the patients should be transferred to another room for more stimulation, the directing psychiatrist agreed and said she had already requested the transfer but the nurses had been unwilling to comply for reasons that were never made clear to her. (Hmmm . . . who's in charge here?)

As soon as I mentioned this problem to a nursing supervisor friend, the transfer immediately took place. As in many areas of life, it's not who you are but who you know! Certainly an example of *inhospitability*!

An 18-year-old female and a 19-year-old male, both diagnosed with depression, were admitted to the inpatient unit within hours of each other. Romeo and Juliet (not their real names) claimed to only vaguely know each other from the neighborhood and, as might seem natural, they immediately became friendly. During breakfast their first morning on the unit, they were observed sitting "too close" to each other, and soon staff concerns about the appropriateness of their behavior became obvious.

Later that morning, in group therapy, Romeo and Juliet expressed mild indignation over the implication that they were anything other than new friends. The discussion hadn't lasted more than a few minutes before Romeo was abruptly summoned out of the group. He returned shortly, having been given the courtesy to come back and tell us he was immediately being transferred to another unit on the basis of a 'rule' that did not permit close (read romantically involved) friends to be treated on the same unit. In another remarkable example of bureaucratic insensitivity, he wasn't even permitted to remain for the rest of the group session during which he might have been able to integrate, understand and perhaps ventilate about this situation.

After he left, Juliet expressed bewilderment, distress, guilt and self-consciousness at presumably being judged to have engaged in some form of inappropriate behavior as well as being the cause of Romeo's transfer. She received much support from the group, particularly from one older man who had been present at breakfast. Along with several other patients, he insisted that only pleasant conversation had occurred between the now star-crossed, non-lovers in a weird approximation of Shakespeare's "Romeo and Juliet". Our Juliet felt somewhat relieved and supported by the group but expressed a sense of alienation from the very staff she had anticipated would offer her objective therapeutic assistance with the difficulties that had precipitated her admission.

Later that same morning, in group therapy on the unit to which Romeo had been transferred, I gave him the opportunity to tell the others what happened. I continued to supportively express my mystification at how rapidly this transfer had taken place, apparently without a careful corroborating review or any discussion with the 'couple', as might have been the more sensitive and therapeutic approach. Everyone reassured Romeo that it appeared from his account that he had done nothing wrong and his concerns about the way he had been treated were valid.

At the afternoon staff meeting I made an attempt to unravel the story. In response to my sharp questioning about the appropriateness of what had transpired for these patients, there were unsubstantiated suggestions that Romeo and Juliet knew each other far better than they had represented, and Romeo had actually gotten himself admitted solely to be with Juliet. The essential allegation here was that they had both been caught in lies. Maybe in *Law and Order*[9] that's how it ends, but in behavioral health that's how it begins.

Informational discrepancies of the kind that apparently existed here should have resulted in subsequent clarification, supportive inquiry and treatment, not moralistic assertions masquerading as objective clinical judgment. In effect, it was the two group therapy sessions that were left to clean up what even the unit chief later admitted had been a serious mistake, possibly in judgment, but certainly in procedure. Just another example of how behavior on the part of well-meaning yet highly pressured staff, chronically anxious about maintaining their (excessively tight) control over patients, became dehumanized in the process.

During a union strike, only the professional staff remained on duty. A female nurse and I were working together on the inpatient unit where a patient with a history of violent behavior was in the Seclusion Area. In fact, this man could be unpleasant even when he wasn't being violent and, at one point, he began demanding to be given a cigarette. (It's unbelievable to look back at that era and recall that patients were actually permitted to smoke on the unit, albeit under the close supervision of a staff member.) The problem was the patient had not completed some routine tasks required of him although he had been repeatedly reminded to do so. The smoking privilege was, therefore, being withheld.

Sulking, the patient finally did what he was told and then demanded his cigarette. Astonishingly, the nurse then countered with what sounded, even to me, like a contrived excuse to further deny his smoking request. He looked at me, pleadingly at first and then progressively more menacingly. Recognizing the no-win situation the nurse had put the patient in, coupled with her obvious expectation that I (the male) would handle any possible ensuing violence, I also looked at her menacingly. Perhaps I shouldn't admit this but, given my irritation with her irresponsibly highhanded manner, for a fleeting moment the possibility of joining with the patient in assaulting her came to mind. Instead, I calmly insisted the nurse let him smoke, which she reluctantly did and the patient and I became buddies forever after.

When a frustrated inpatient once referred to his psychiatrist as "Dr. Mengele",[10] instead of seeing this as most likely the patient's projected anger and responding professionally by reflecting that back to the patient, the psychiatrist became outraged at the insult (Was there a grain of truth in it?), and demanded an immediate apology, which only added to the patient's distress and further undermined what was already a minimal psychological support system on that unit.

In the day treatment service, we once had a patient who needed immediate involuntary hospitalization. Anticipating his active resistance, the staff cautiously surrounded him in preparation for applying restraints but, as soon as the patient became aware of what was about to happen, he made a dash for the stairs. One of our psychiatrists chased him down the hall and tackled him to the floor whereupon other staff then restrained and transported the patient to the inpatient unit.

In the subsequent clinical meeting where the case was discussed, this psychiatrist referred to the patient as having been "violent" during the incident. I felt compelled to point out to him, as well as the rest of the staff who were nodding their heads in agreement, that the only person who had actually been "violent" was the psychiatrist with his tackle and take down. The patient had harmed no one and was simply trying to escape. The written record was set straight, avoiding any erroneous documentation that the patient had been violent. I cite this as an example of how easily misleading and distorted information can negatively impact the treatment of patients.

Finally, reminiscent of the infamous Dreyfus Affair,[11] I'll never forget the patient who announced in a group therapy session that the staff had "*accused*" him of being a schizophrenic!

Notes

1   This is an extremely complex novel written by James Joyce, initially published serially and then in its entirety in 1922.
2   Written by Pete Seeger and released in 1962. (The lyrics were adapted from the Book of Ecclesiastes.)
3   The middle part of the classic American folk tune "I've Been Working on the Railroad", 1894.
4   Written by the Australian hard rock band AC/DC.
5   Written by June Carter Cash, wife of Johnny Cash, about their relationship. Released in 1963.

6 A 1987 single by the Grateful Dead from their album *In the Dark*. It was composed by Jerry Garcia with lyrics by Robert Hunter and is known for its refrain "I will get by / I will survive".

7 With apologies to Rene Descartes, whose original phrase, *je pense, donc je suis* (I think therefore I am) which appeared in his *Discourse on the Method* (1637) or *cogito ergo sum* in the *Principles of Philosophy* (1644).

8 A common reference to restraints applied to both arms and both legs.

9 NBC TV series filmed between 1990 and 2010 and currently widely shown in reruns.

10 Josef Mengele, nicknamed 'The Angel of Death', was a notorious physician in a Nazi concentration camp during World War II who selected prisoners for cruel and often fatal medical experiments, as well as for extermination.

11 Alfred Dreyfus was a Jewish French Artillery captain falsely accused of passing military secrets to the Germans. He was officially exonerated in 1906.

Chapter 6

Patient deaths

Suicide

Whether completed or merely attempted, suicide is surely the most dreaded of treatment outcomes, the implication being there was some failure on the part of the treating clinician(s). Hospitals refer to patient suicides as "sentinel events", and every completed suicide necessitates a formal, postmortem investigation known as a "Root Cause Analysis". Conducted by a committee convened by the risk management department, the purpose of these reviews is to determine if any *systemic* failures contributed to the outcome. In a perfect world these investigations are an opportunity for everyone to learn from the event, but the potential always exists they will turn into witch-hunts, thus enabling leadership to cover themselves at the expense of the treating clinicians. It has been my observation that the staff is too frequently considered guilty until proven innocent.

At one such Root Cause Analysis meeting, a hospital administrator verbally excoriated the staff for not preventing the patient's suicide. In response, a physician member of the review committee spoke out in defense of the treating clinicians. He said:

> When I treat a patient with a bad heart, and the patient eventually and inevitably dies, no one questions my treatment. Similarly, this should be true in behavioral health. They do the best they can but there are times when no intervention can prevent what turns out to be an unavoidable consequence.

The accusatorial administrator was someone with a background in treating the mentally ill, so we might have expected her to know better but she never deviated from her critical, judgmental tone despite the lack of any evidence to support a lapse in treatment protocol. She apparently could not bring herself to publicly concede that when treating patients at high risk for suicide, as noted by a history of serious prior attempts, some will eventually succeed. Often overlooked is any acknowledgment that up to that time the clinicians had successfully managed to extend the life of this patient. That particular Root *canal* . . ., uh, Root *Cause* Analysis, meeting was for one completed suicide among a number of cases that had occurred over the previous three years in the day treatment service: One patient jumped off a building after eloping[1] from the inpatient unit while transitioning to day treatment.

Another was found dead under a bridge. One man apparently drowned himself in the harbor although his family remained convinced he had been murdered. Another woman survived a previous attempt, 25 years earlier, when she jumped from a building holding her infant. The infant was killed. This time when she jumped, she killed herself. Two other patients had jumped in front of subway cars but managed to survive.

Against the very large number of high-risk patients we treated, these 'failures' statistically constituted a very small percentage. Nevertheless, the ever self-protective administration identified these deaths as a 'cluster' because of their apparent temporal proximity, and brought in an Ivy League 'expert' to evaluate our handling of these cases. He found we had met the highest standards of care only to face the occasionally inevitable consequence of treating patients at high risk for suicide. This exoneration relieved and delighted the 'not guilty' day treatment staff.

At a subsequent meeting related to the 'expert's' evaluation, a department supervisor asked why we admitted such high-risk patients to our program when they lived quite far away from the hospital. (The day treatment service, unlike the inpatient psychiatric service, was not subject to any geographic catchment area.) "Isn't that our mission?" I wondered aloud. Was he actually suggesting we cherry-pick only low- or no-risk patients for admission?

"Just kidding!" he said, quickly backtracking.

Some people find humor in the strangest situations.

One of these suicides was a very bright female with a diagnosis of schizophrenia and an extensive psychiatric history that included many years of psychotherapy, medications and numerous hospitalizations. The pattern of her illness was recurring decompensations[2] followed by restoration to health for a period of time, each episode leaving her somewhat encouraged that her illness had finally abated. Now, however, she was once again on our inpatient unit, under constant observation by a psychology intern. Tragically, she managed to escape from the unit and jump to her death from the roof of a nearby building. The pain of such volatility had finally become unbearable, leaving her unable to sustain hope of ever achieving lasting stability.

The intern was devastated by this outcome and required a great deal of emotional support to deal with his grief and guilt. Helping him enabled me to resolve some of my own sorrow over her death.

Some time after day treatment had been reduced to a much more limited program due to substantial defunding, a recently discharged patient, one considered to be high risk for suicide, jumped off a roof to his death. At the requisite postmortem conference, his medical record was reviewed and revealed he had previously attempted suicide after being discharged from the inpatient unit. The patient had subsequently told his therapist it was *the loss of the therapeutic community* he had found within the former day treatment service that precipitated his (failed) attempt. Quite likely that same factor played a significant role in his ultimately successful suicide.

And then there was the chronically psychotic patient desperately in need of treatment who had remained non-compliant despite our numerous initiatives. Once, when we visited his apartment, we found it in complete disarray. Even his dog seemed psychotic! Subsequently, on a day when the temperature soared into the 90s, the patient was found wrapped in numerous blankets, dead apparently of heat stroke and dehydration.

Violence

With the help of a partner and poor judgment, a very likeable young male patient in day treatment, one who was also a drug dealer, attempted to steal money from a customer who turned out to be a cop. During this drug deal-gone-bad, the patient and his partner were shot and killed.

A psychotic male patient was persistent in battering his wife (also a patient). Although we urged her many times to leave him, she never did. Eventually he fractured her skull, and was arrested and jailed in a city prison where he died under mysterious circumstances. Had his reputation followed him?

Natural causes

A long-term day treatment patient and I shared a running gag. Whenever we were together in the unit's recreation area, he would quip: "What's up, doc?" My standard reply: "Only my proctologist knows!" This never failed to elicit his appreciative laughter.

Gradually his overall physical health began to deteriorate and, after a brief period of absence from day treatment, he turned up in the emergency department. Recognizing that his prognosis was grim, he asked for help in drawing up a will so he could leave his money, a substantial sum apparently, to some close patient-friends. Given the emergency nature of the situation, hospital administration was asked to provide him with an in-house lawyer but they refused, citing a potential conflict of interest. Since there was little time for the patient to get his own lawyer, we affected an informal will in accordance with his 'dying declaration'. Sadly, however, for reasons beyond our control, and in the absence of any known family, the city marshals took custody of all his possessions and assets. Thus, his final wishes were disregarded.

Deaths due medical causes are relatively rare on inpatient psychiatry units, but I recall a male patient who suffered an apparent cardiac arrest. Resuscitation efforts by the 'code' team were unsuccessful and the naked body (except for the black socks on his feet) was left on the floor (where resuscitation is often attempted because it is the only available firm surface). A mental health worker and I placed the body back on the bed and I remained alone with the corpse, in the absolute and stark silence of the room, to fill out the toe tag[3] and tie it on the toe of the corpse.

It was a very surreal experience. (Is there a standard knot for this procedure?)

Notes

1 A term used when patients leave without proper authorization.
2 Psychiatrese for deterioration/decline.
3 "A piece of cardboard normally attached with string to the big toe of a dead body. It is used for identification purposes, allowing the mortician, coroner, law enforcement and others involved in the death process to correctly identify the corpse." Wikipedia.

Chapter 7

Staff partings

Expiration dates

The departure of colleagues is sad to witness whether resulting from resignations, layoffs (due to the relentless reduction in funding), terminations for cause, retirement or death. As a supervisor, even when I knew the termination was appropriate or inevitable, I always found it difficult to deal with.

A married, management level staff member demonstrated a serious lapse in judgment when he engaged in a very flagrant affair with a nurse under his supervision. I had no recourse but to recommend he be terminated because the staff no longer had confidence in him.

A patient on our day treatment service revealed she had had consensual sex with a mental health worker and her story carried the ring of truth. Administration was informed and the mental health worker was confronted. He readily admitted he had been to the patient's home "at least once" but said it was only for the purpose of "fixing the lock on her door". (His detailed description of the process reeked of symbolism and obfuscation.)

In the interest of our patients' welfare, it was decided his termination was essential. A union arbitration hearing subsequently restored his job on the grounds there was no objective evidence of any extracurricular involvement with the patient, only her anecdotal account. The mental health worker was, however, never allowed to work with patients again and eventually he left to take a job as an armed security guard.

He came back for a visit once, in uniform and with a holstered revolver prominently displayed on his hip. Probably he just wanted to show us he had salvaged his self-esteem rather than shoot us, but I do think he exposed the gun as a kind of a sardonic tease.

I should also add there was the confounding factor of race: the staff member was African-American and the patient was white. A good friend and colleague, an African-American woman, was convinced there had been a "lynching" of this "innocent" African-American man. Sadly, this turned out to be the end of our friendship.

Two essentially conscientious and capable staff members were found to have continued writing progress notes on a patient despite the fact that she had died seven months earlier. We learned of this when the patient's husband called to ask why he was being billed for treatment for his dead wife. The clinicians' assertions that they were pressured to do this by supervisors were not credible and never validated. That is not to say the staff wasn't under enormous pressure for productivity, irrespective of the quality of their work, so their view of the clinical work environment was not unrealistic and undoubtedly contributed to their impaired judgment. This time there was substantial objective evidence and the decision to terminate was sustained by arbitration. To their credit, department leadership tried to limit the sanctions to some sort of extended suspension; upper level management, however, in their characteristically CYA (cover your [their] ass) style, insisted they be fired. (Claims that we never give up on a patient would probably not have gotten us very far.)

There were other terminations that I found even more unsettling. One was the staff psychiatrist whose erratic behavior was initially seen by the director of her service as simply evidence of fatigue, with no intervention required. Eventually she was found standing on a radiator in a patient's room exclaiming that rays were passing through her body.

Instead of supporting her, perhaps even urging her to take a medical leave, management offered her a letter of recommendation in exchange for her immediate resignation. Certainly this raised ethical issues, but apparently her mental illness was considered an embarrassment to us.

Another disturbing episode involved a social worker chronically late in obtaining the state-required signatures of his intellectually limited patients on their treatment plans. He was eventually caught forging a number of their signatures, and this resulted in his termination. Foolishly, instead of making these bogus signatures look like something a limited person might write, the social worker had signed them with a highly sophisticated flourish, in a handwriting that could in no way have been produced by his patients. Apparently he was contemptuously venting his anger at the enormous pressure he was under, and perhaps the humiliation to which he felt he had been subjected. Maybe he simply wanted out.

One of our psychologists was once caught leaving the hospital with a box of paper goods he had taken from the inpatient unit. He tried to make the case they were for use at a non-profit event, but that didn't work and he was summarily fired.

In my private practice I have also helped people deal with work-related disciplinary actions. One case involved a medical resident I was treating for social skills and relationship issues, as well as mild depression. In our session one day, she told me about a teenager who had died in the emergency department as a direct result, she said, of the delayed response of an attending physician. At the hospital she had been outspoken in her criticism of the way the case was handled and, apparently in retaliation, it was reported to the state medical society that she had a diagnosis of attention deficit hyperactivity disorder (ADHD), something I never saw any clinical evidence of.

A committee of the state medical society then stipulated she undergo an evaluation by a psychiatrist and she agreed to this. The psychiatrist found no evidence to support a diagnosis of ADHD, however, his written report listed diagnoses of mood disorder, anxiety disorder and possible "bipolar spectrum disorder", all based on his one 50-minute evaluation. He recommended ongoing assessment of the resident, in the context of psychiatric treatment, along with practice monitoring, and a period of urine toxicology screening to rule out any substance abuse, even though there had never been any history, nor even prior mention, of such a problem. This regimen was to be carried out under the aegis of the committee and, according to the resident, the overview was to last for three years.

The committee had also specified she ask a number of her friends, relatives and colleagues to complete Attention Deficit Disorder (ADD) checklists.[1] The results of these were all negative.

For reasons never made clear, the committee also 'requested' that she undergo a neuropsychological examination, at her own expense, of approximately $3,000. This she refused.

Understandably, she felt harassed and humiliated by these requirements and they clearly contributed to her overall impression of arbitrary and unfair treatment. This apparent attempt to discredit her would seriously impair her professional future. She felt it was clear she had antagonized the wrong people by not handling the situation more tactfully, but she couldn't understand the prolonged personal antipathy. She didn't even know who had reported her to the committee as her supervisors remained evasive on the matter. Although she had previously been cautioned about her aggressive style, there had never been any accusation of medical incompetence. In fact, her supervising senior resident had only recently documented her overall excellent work.

I advised her to consult an attorney, as well as her union representative, and not sign any papers without first consulting them. As well, with her permission, I spoke to the committee case manager on her behalf and made the following points:

1   Apparently one of her physician supervisors with a clear conflict of interest made the initial gratuitous judgment of ADHD even though not qualified to make a *psychiatric* diagnosis.
2   I suggested that the reporting individual be urged to make her or himself known if there was any genuine concern for the resident's welfare.
3   This diagnosis was conveyed to the committee without the resident's permission, clearly unethical and probably illegal. I would, therefore, consider filing my own complaint about this matter to the appropriate authorities.
4   The psychiatric evaluation recommended by the committee was very brief and thus the findings could only be considered imprecise at best and not ethically applicable, particularly in view of the potential and needless damage to a promising career.

The case manager apparently agreed with my points and almost immediately the resident received a letter from the committee effectively exonerating her and indicating the case would be closed. They wished her the best in her medical career.

While I can't be certain about the precise effect of my phone call, or what other factors might have contributed to this favorable outcome, the temporal proximity of my call to the letter suggests it had at least some influence. The entire episode lasted about six weeks so justice was delayed but not denied![2]

Notes

1   D. G. Amen, *Adult ADD Symptom Checklist*, Irvine, CA: MindWorks Press, 1998.
2   Again with apologies to William Gladstone, British politician, 1809–1898. "Justice delayed is justice denied." Address to Parliament on the adoption of the disestablishment of the Church of Ireland as a policy of the Liberal Party, on 16 March 1868.

Chapter 8

Psychotherapy

Conventional, evidence-based psychotherapy with individuals, couples, families or groups is labor-intensive and time consuming. Thus, it is continually at odds with the demands of patients as well as insurance companies, for the quick, relatively easy fixes anticipated from medication. The expected outcome of treatment appears to be low-cost symptom-reduction realized as quickly as possible. Inadequate attention is paid to the underlying problems, thus relapse is a not uncommon result.

In psychotherapy, an "empathic"[1] context enables patients to hear and understand what they are really saying; it is crucial to success In their book *Second-Order Change in Psychotherapy*, Salovey and Fraser conclude: "Client-therapist relationship factors, a positive working alliance, and other common therapeutic factors . . . such as warmth, empathy and acceptance, encouragement of risk taking . . . account for the vast majority of influences on positive therapy outcome".[2] In other words, the *relationship* is a critical aspect of the intervention.

In my experience, the judicious use of humor is helpful in setting a comfortable tone for patients, no matter what the psychotherapeutic setting. As well, it provides patients with a model for risk-taking. The anxiety often associated with an expectation of formality may be reduced as a more relaxed, non-judgmental ambience is promoted.

Patients often have fixed beliefs that hinder the development of insight. An old story that underscores the difficulty of challenging these beliefs concerns a patient who was convinced he was dead.[3] The patient had been in treatment for several years yet, no matter how much evidence or logic the doctor applied, the patient was not dissuaded. Finally the psychiatrist had what he thought was a brilliant idea: He asked the patient if dead people bleed. "Of course not!" the patient replied. The psychiatrist then picked up a scalpel and pricked the patient's finger producing a large drop of blood. "What do you have to say about that?" asked the psychiatrist. The patient replied, "What do you know, dead people bleed."[4]

Blaming others for most of their difficulties is a common obstacle many patients need to overcome in order to gain insight. Fritz Perls, a distinguished psychiatrist, put it this way: "We live in a house of mirrors and think we are looking out of windows."[5]

The relentless assault of overwhelmingly disastrous, seemingly out-of-control worldwide events, made more immediate and inescapable by today's expanding information technology, seems to have lessened any expectation of reliable societal stability for many patients. With increasing frequency, I have seen such concerns woven into an individual's presenting problems and it appears to me that we may be approaching the globalization of what is called "Generalized Anxiety Disorder" in the *Diagnostic and Statistical Manual of Mental Disorders*.[6]

Individual

An attractive, well-groomed young man came to my office complaining of anxiety. While taking his history, he told me he worked as a 'book maker'. "Oh, you work in a bindery?" I naively asked. "No . . . I take bets!" he said, his facial expression implying I was an idiot.

Over the course of his treatment he offered me numerous tips on horse races, all of which I graciously and ethically declined. (No, I really did!)

Over an extended period of time I treated a tall, laconic man in his 60s. His diagnosis was paranoid schizophrenia with obsessive and compulsive features. He was very intelligent and had a sardonic, sophisticated wit he mercilessly applied to himself and others in equal measure. He was able to smile when he felt something was genuinely humorous but his smile betrayed his underlying sadness. Having spent many years in a state hospital he was actually proud of his diagnosis, referring to himself as a "professional mental patient". He often related, with a mixture of genuine dignity and slight bemusement, that this was the 23rd year in his "distinguished career". The 'professionalism' with which he approached his "vocation" of mental illness masked the fact that he had long ago given up any hope of recovery or significant improvement in his life.

He had always been dependent on his mother and after her death he became even more helpless. Living alone in a small apartment (in the days before self-defrosting freezers), he was unable to bring himself to defrost his refrigerator. He could only watch as more and more ice formed until he was unable to close the freezer door. When encouraged to do something, he would just shrug his shoulders.

He occasionally alluded to numerous rituals he followed, but declined to describe most of them. He confessed he consumed large quantities of granulated sugar, spooning it right out of a five-pound bag. He loved to walk, for miles at a time. Once he told me he had walked from the city to an outer suburb and back, all in one day. He was also a chain smoker. Overall, however, his life was grim drudgery.

Periodically he would express concerns about his sexuality, often describing fantasies about the housekeepers sent by social services. (Apparently none of them were willing to defrost his freezer.) Invariably they were "colored" women from the "islands", of substantial "Rubenesque" proportions. He particularly dwelt, in extensive detail, on the *"roundness"* of these women. He described fantasized, and actual but doomed, attempts at seduction. His voice would deepen and his intellectual detachment would vanish. As he spoke, he stared straight ahead, as if he could see them in the room. He would become visibly flushed, this fantasy offering him at least a moment of escape from the psychological constrictions that encased him.

Interestingly, he was also preoccupied with his own body and a fear that if he ate too much (never worrying, apparently, about the large amounts of sugar he was consuming), he would develop a roundness attractive to other men. He often talked about fantasies of inserting carrots and cucumbers into his rectum, underlining his anxiety that he was, after all, really a homosexual. No amount of reassurance or reminders of his interest in his female housekeepers helped.

One day when he started his litany about the carrots and cucumbers signifying his homosexuality, I turned to him in desperation and said, "You're not a homosexual, you're a vegetarian!" A moment of stunned silence followed, and then he broke out in hearty laughter. Subsequently this preoccupation seemed to loosen its hold on him and he mentioned it less and less frequently.

While treating a fellow mental health professional with a history of serious mental illness and related hospitalizations, she turned to me during the session one day and condescendingly offered a bit of free 'supervision': "I don't think I would have said that to me at this point."

After filing insurance claim forms for a patient I had been treating for a number of years, the insurance company erroneously reimbursed her directly rather than sending the check to me. At the time, she neglected to tell me this.

On the evening the patient arrived for what turned out to be our last session, she was carrying a beautiful, full-sized toboggan. Confessing she had just shoplifted it from a department store, she propped it against the waiting room wall and came into my office for her session.

When closing up later that evening, there was the toboggan still in my waiting room. Had the patient left it for me instead of the insurance check to which she knew I was entitled? Although I made several attempts to contact her, it wasn't until two years later that I finally heard from her. She sent me a check for the full payment, along with a very sweet note of apology saying she had desperately needed the money at that time for living expenses. The toboggan was not mentioned.

A well-spoken middle-aged woman called to request a consultation with me. We met and she coherently, logically and with appropriate affect recounted how as a very young child in Europe her mother periodically dropped her off at "orgies" where men sexually abused her. She described being tortured and humiliated, alternately assaulted and paradoxically protected throughout the course of this abuse. Eventually, in her early adolescence, she was coerced into performing the worst kind of violent act as a condition of gaining her own freedom; presumably having this horrific act hanging over her head would keep her quiet, and it did.

At the time I saw her, she gave no overt evidence of any psychopathology that might have called into question the veracity of these astonishing revelations. Prior to coming to me, she had undergone several years of psychotherapy with another therapist. Although this had helped with the enormity of her guilt, she never completely got over feeling that she did not deserve anything positive in her life. This was reminiscent of the 'survivor guilt' experienced by Holocaust victims who had to steal food and clothing from other prisoners in order to stay alive.

During that initial hour we explored the patient's difficulties and I offered as much reassurance and support as an hour would allow. This turned out to be our only meeting; the patient felt this brief contact was sufficient for the moment, and she seemed reassured just to know I was there in the event of future need.

Another patient I met with only briefly was an anorexic woman who always wore a cap on her head and reluctantly admitted she plucked every single hair out of every part of her body. After establishing some degree of trust with her, she finally took off her head covering to reveal complete baldness. My recollection is that she left treatment shortly after that exposure, despite what I thought was my unequivocal acceptance of her appearance. Perhaps, however, that was the problem!

Couples

A woman and her significant other came to see me for couples counseling. They wanted to work out some issues in their relationship, even though he was still married to someone else. He was very successful in the commercial home improvement business and although he never discussed business-related matters with me, eventually it emerged that he had ties to organized crime and was currently looking over his shoulder at serious threats. After a number of bodies were found buried in the work yard at his place of business, he entered the government witness protection program in exchange for his eventual testimony in a number of mob related trials.

A concern unique to this psychotherapy relationship was the paper trail created by the checks drawn on his business account to pay me for therapy. A legitimate uneasiness of mine, a fear actually, was that one of his 'colleagues' with access to his records and a score to settle might think I would know where to find him. So, in case anyone reading this is looking for him (or me), I know nothing.

An angry, pregnant Orthodox Jewish woman wanted a 'therapeutic abortion'[7] (the only legal kind prior to Roe v. Wade in 1973). She came to see me in the outpatient clinic with her husband; she wanted a divorce because he was not sexually satisfying her, a requirement of Jewish law. They had once tried a variation of the traditional missionary position and although this position was much more satisfying for her, it was against Jewish law so the husband refused to repeat the practice. The question I posed to him was: "Do you want to be right or do you want your marriage? Either way you're violating Jewish law so why not violate the law in the way that least harms your marriage?"

He immediately agreed with this formulation, but it was necessary to get permission from their rabbi first. The rabbi agreed and their marriage was saved. Several months later they came to show me their new baby.

Many years ago I conducted a 'marital' therapy session with three people who considered themselves married to each other. A second man had joined the original couple, but now they were experiencing difficulties. During the initial (and only) interview with all three present, I asked how their sexual relationship was conducted. Did they all have sex together, I wondered? Looking at me with utter contempt, they chorused: "No! That would be sick!" Apparently the idea had never occurred to them; it was always one man at a time while the other waited his turn. They said this with great principled authority, giving the expression "three's a crowd" new meaning. "Sounds lonely for the other guy," I speculated, my moral standing now apparently in question. I never saw them again.

A 40-something social worker with depression had been in therapy with me for a number of months. She complained of intensifying loneliness as she slowly and with great difficulty went through the process of extricating herself from a destructive relationship with a man who had been exploiting her. When that relationship was finally over, she ended therapy.

Several years passed and then she came to see me again with a painful new difficulty. She had met a "wonderful" man and developed a deep romantic attachment to him. Then he was diagnosed with terminal leukemia and once the treatments became too difficult for him, he decided suicide was his only recourse. Overwhelmingly saddened, she nevertheless lovingly helped with his preparations, even assisting him in writing his suicide note. After telling her she would hear about him in few days, he had climbed into his van, with his handgun, and driven away. She did not immediately learn what had become of him but consulted me for help in dealing with her intense grief.

Finally, a few weeks later, she came across a newspaper account: police at a local airport had found his body inside his parked van, a single bullet wound to his head. Sadly, this gave new meaning to *Long Term Parking*!

A well-educated, upper middle class couple started therapy in an attempt to deal with their domestic violence issues; mainly it was she who assaulted him, mostly on the weekends. Despite their obvious commitment to therapy, they proved resistant to change and it remained clear they did not want to separate. He continued to say the things that provoked her, and she continued to assault him.

When I learned of his sudden death due to an apparent heart attack, his wife's assaultive behaviors came to mind as a possible contributing factor. I telephoned to offer my condolences, but the answering machine picked up and it was his voice on the outgoing message. It felt a bit eerie, and I imagined him saying, "Hello. I'm dead now but you can leave a message for my wife."

Then there was the married woman who reported, in our initial interview, that she had discovered panties in her bedroom that were not hers. She convinced herself her husband was having an affair but when she finally confronted him and he admitted he was a transvestite, she found this far more disturbing than if he had actually been having an extramarital relationship.

Learning of his sexual deviation prompted her to seek help but as I only saw her for one or two sessions, I don't know what eventually happened to the marriage. By helping reduce her initial shock and anxiety, however, she was able to begin to put this trauma into perspective.

9/11 – World Trade Center trauma

Before the terrorist attacks on the World Trade Center (WTC) in 2001, I was treating a woman who worked at a human services agency located across the street from the Twin Towers. Through a window in her office, she watched as the planes crashed into the buildings.

Subsequently she was too traumatized to immediately return to work yet the commissioner of this agency threatened her with loss of her job if she didn't report directly back to the office. An excerpt of the letter I wrote on her behalf speaks to the inhumanity of that organization:

> I evaluated and treated Ms. J. on the evening of October 1, 2001 in response to an urgent call from her. She described her experience on Tuesday, September 11th in graphic detail. She was working in a building very close to the World Trade Center, on an upper floor where she witnessed the collisions and subsequent events. She reported that her floor was soon filled with smoke and that she received contradictory directions from supervisors about whether or not to immediately vacate the building. Finally exiting, she witnessed additional horrible events on the street, eventually making her way to the ferry that took her over to Staten Island. From there she walked back to the Verrazano Bridge and then waited several hours before a bus took her to the Brooklyn side where she was left to eventually be picked up by her daughter. . . . (She) reports experiencing intense anxiety since that day which is exacerbated by any event-related precipitant and she is particularly resistant to returning to her work site. . . . I recommend that (she) be given every consideration with respect to her work environment, both physical and psychological, which should be sensitive to her current level of distress and be conducive to her eventual recovery.

The commissioner relented, and she was able to keep her job.

After the attacks, I treated two former firefighters who lost many colleagues. They had spent numerous days digging at Ground Zero, carrying out bodies of victims, many of whom they had personally known. One lost 15 of his firefighter friends but apparently was never offered proper counseling by the Fire Department. He resorted to alcohol abuse and cocaine use, the possession of which eventually led to his arrest. Although the charges were dropped and he attended rehab, the Fire Commissioner terminated him several years after the tragedy, denying him any pension. At his termination hearing my concluding remarks summarized his situation:

> Given the severity of his diagnoses (PTSD and major depression) and the paucity of treatment initially offered by the Fire Department, it is clear that the onset of his substance abuse, proximate to these events, was a clear attempt at self-medication in order to find relief from both the above noted symptoms as well as the recurrent, graphic memories of the WTC horrors and immediate outcomes.

The diagnosis of PTSD was somewhat of an understatement, but both firefighters eventually did well in confronting and at least partially resolving some of the emotional sequelae of their experiences. It is worth noting that the firefighter who experienced actual job loss and the patient who was only threatened with job loss at the human services agency, both served under the same individual who was variously commissioner of the Fire Department and the human services agency.

Another patient I saw for therapy had worked as a high-level computer technician in one of the WTC towers. On 9/11 he was late getting to work but arrived just in time to see the first plane strike. He witnessed people jumping out of windows and other horrific sights he could never forget but had great difficulty talking about. Compounding his emotional difficulties and adding to his overall distress was the immediate loss of his tech job as a result of the attacks.

At the time of his therapy he was working as a public school teacher but eventually lost that job because of uncontrolled anger he directed at his young students. He had little insight into the relationship between his anger, his resentment at being a teacher and his experiences on 9/11, continuing instead to blame his feelings on the behavior of the children.

Despite the opportunity psychotherapy afforded him to ventilate, during the time of treatment he was never able to gain any substantial understanding of the traumatic source of his anger.

Civil service trauma

For an extended period of time I treated a middle-aged African-American woman who worked as a 'housing assistant' in a public housing project. Caught in the cross fire of a gang fight, she sustained several bullet wounds to her abdomen resulting in the need for multiple surgeries, long-term medical treatment and an ongoing fear of returning to work.

She was diagnosed with PTSD and eventually assigned a desk job at a central headquarters building.

During treatment she spoke of the initial trauma. She suffered from recurrent dreams, experienced night sweats and flashbacks, often precipitated by news reports of shootings.

She developed a chronic paranoid fear of any young black man she saw on the street and would cross to the other side to avoid him.

She became convinced the people in her office were deliberately using air fresheners to which they knew she was allergic, causing many outbursts at work and her ultimate isolation from co-workers. With a pre-incident history of being disciplined for inappropriate remarks, it appears the traumatic incident served to exacerbate previous problems. She developed a reclusive existence, only visiting her extended family in other states on rare occasions.

Against her wishes, she eventually returned to a field position where the deaths of tenants saddened her. Handling her role in the eviction of tenants was very difficult.

Over the many years she was in treatment, she received considerable support in dealing with these stresses. Although she was helped to hold on to her job and to cope with the administrative rigidities she faced there, insight into her paranoid sensitivities, as noted above, was never gained by the time she terminated treatment.

A police officer who suffered from an acute anxiety disorder had spent the better part of his career managing to stay one step ahead of an ongoing commission investigating police corruption. In treatment he spoke of a common late night practice where he and his partner would erect a temporary, cash only tollbooth on one of the city's bridges. Under cover of darkness (and with minimal supervision), they simply pocketed all the unrecorded revenue that flowed from the faux tollbooth!

Another police officer I saw was assigned to desk duty and told me his badge and gun were taken away as a result of complaints he made at work about imagined police surveillance, harassment and his assumption that the department disapproved of his interracial marriage. In order to be restored to full duty, he was told he needed to undergo psychotherapy, with an eventual positive outcome, before he could have his gun returned.

He had a history of excellent functioning in all previous employment settings, no work related problems, not even during the period of his current difficulties, and no indication he continued to sustain those beliefs. He had no psychiatric history, had never been on any psychiatric medication, and mental status examination as well as all psychological tests were negative for any current psychopathology. He appeared motivated for psychotherapy.

In his treatment, we focused on an exploration of what had led to his imagined concerns at work and, gradually over a period of several months, he gained substantial insight.

When the police department eventually asked for my clinical impressions, I provided an extensively detailed report concluding with my judgment that this police officer could be safely restored to full duty. Despite the initial promise by his supervisor that he would be restored to duty pending the successful outcome of psychotherapy, they now sought the opinion of a psychiatrist.

In follow-up discussions I had with the police psychologist monitoring this case, it became clear to me there was substantial resistance within the police department to returning a weapon to an officer assessed with a psychiatric disorder, irrespective of subsequent treatment outcome. Given what had happened, they felt they could never be confident that some stressor wouldn't again 'trigger' the patient's capacity for distortion.

It also became clear that this police psychologist's overriding concern was the possibility that any shooting or other comparable incident the officer might be involved in in the future would undoubtedly come back to bite her, no matter the circumstances. Self-protection (aka CYA) was clearly one of the highest priorities in this police department. I came to understand that the department had always anticipated my patient's eventual termination, even if he successfully met their requirements. One might ask, why the need for this prolonged and misleading process?

Another example of bureaucratic callousness involved a prison guard who had sustained two successive beatings by prisoners using iron pipes, resulting in significant traumatic brain damage. At the request of his attorneys, I saw the patient several times in order to conduct a thorough examination. They were arguing with the city over the degree of traumatic brain injury, the city attorneys maintaining the prison guard was not as significantly impaired as was alleged.

A health aide always accompanied the patient to my office. Unassisted it is doubtful he could have found his way in or out, let alone have traveled there by himself. Of necessity our sessions were abbreviated as he had a short attention span, poor concentration and was easily fatigued. This alone was sufficient to make the case for significant impairment. My examination revealed substantial cognitive damage secondary to the successive traumas.

Eventually the city offered the patient a settlement, but it was far from commensurate with the pain, suffering and permanent disability he had experienced.

I once treated a man who told me he was a police officer as well as a former member of the US Special Forces. There was no basis at the time for me to question the veracity of his account. The goal of treatment was to help him learn to control his anger toward his wife, also a police officer, who had filed for divorce.

Several months later, he was arrested and charged with the murder of his wife. His story to me was that she had shot herself in front of him and their child, but he was eventually found guilty and given a sentence of life imprisonment. The trial was well covered in the press and that's where I learned he was neither a police officer nor a former member of Special Forces. Later I learned he had won an appeal on the basis of a technicality, however, he remained in prison with the appeal, at least temporarily, overturned.

Inpatient groups

Facilitating group therapy on an acute, short length-of-stay inpatient unit is unique among all the psychotherapies. As noted by Irving Yalom, a well-respected existential psychiatrist, expert on psychotherapy and author,[8] each session comprises a challenging new group. Of necessity, there is usually a 'here and now' orientation in these groups and, for the most part, the patients are emotionally distracted and cognitively disorganized. Rapid, continuous assessment by the therapist, with immediate identification of underlying themes, is required. This process can result in improved overall clinical acuity and sensitivity for the clinician, essentially a 'psychotherapy' gym! As much as possible, patients are encouraged to look at their interactions with each other as a basis for understanding the self-defeating behaviors that contribute to their interpersonal dysfunction. Ideally, they gain sufficient insight during the session to effect changes in behavior, thus helping them cope more effectively outside the hospital, and reducing the likelihood of relapse.

Here are a few examples of how humor can be used to defuse a potentially difficult situation: During a group comprised primarily of some very surly male characters, a man dressed in religious attire angrily confronted me, and biblically demanded, "What do you think of 'Eye for an Eye'?" I responded, "I like all the vowels!" which both surprised and amused several of these men and resulted in a consequent reduction in the overall tension in the group.

Similarly, after a patient in another group dryly recited his problems listing them as A, B, C and D, a good-natured cynic in the group asked, "Why do the letters of the alphabet have to be in that order? Why can't we re-order them in different ways?" My response: "We do. They're called 'words'!"

I was once asked if I believed in reincarnation. My answer was: "I did in a previous life but not anymore." This remark elicited some laughter, but also prompted a number of people in the group to actually question and talk about some of their own magical assumptions about life and death.

During a group discussion of sexual issues, a patient noted he often had the impulse to expose himself and occasionally acted on these impulses. He also told the group that he regularly used Viagra, even while here on the inpatient unit. When asked how he could afford this expensive medication usually not covered by Medicaid, he responded that he had pleaded 'hardship'. "Shouldn't that have been 'soft-ship'?" I quietly asked. The group laughed and this remark actually had the positive effect of reducing the group's hesitancy to discuss sexual matters.

A patient in another group said he believed he was a spy for the Mossad.[9] It was pointed out to him that if he were really a spy, he wouldn't be telling us this. "All right," he said, "So I'm a poor spy!" He laughed with the group and it subsequently appeared he let go of this delusion as a consequence of the exchange.

There was once a depressed young woman, with a history of drug abuse and much self-hatred, who had attempted suicide the previous summer by swallowing anti-freeze. She nearly died, and ingesting that liquid had to have been a harrowing experience. During the discussion, the suggestion was made that perhaps she had an intense need to painfully punish herself. She agreed and acknowledged this experience had been agonizing. Expressing appreciation for all the support she had just received from the group, she was finally even able to laugh when I observed, with mock incredulity: "Anti-freeze in *August*?"

Then there was the man who revealed to the group that he had served 20 years in prison for committing a double homicide. "Twins?" I asked. The patient, a surprisingly good-natured guy, laughed along with the group thus attenuating the anxiety others might have attached to having a murderer in their midst.

In another group a patient once confessed to worrying about getting older. As someone of more advanced years, I retorted that I worried about not getting older!

During a group therapy session one day, the patients were discussing the importance of remaining focused on the present with minimal concern for the past or anxiety about the uncertainty of the future. One patient went so far as to say that one should completely forget the past and certainly shouldn't dwell at all on the future. One should remain in the moment and only in the moment, she said, "Just focus on the moment." When asked why she was admitted to the hospital, she said that she had forgotten who she was!

A middle-aged man was admitted to the inpatient unit after walking around the streets naked in rather inclement and frosty weather. Despite the best efforts of the group members to convince him otherwise, he saw no problem with this behavior. It wasn't until I said to him, "Man, you have to have pockets!" At that, as if he finally seemed to get it, he exclaimed: "Yes! That's right!"

In a group consisting mostly of patients with auditory hallucinations (among other symptoms), there was one woman who complained of "little green men" all over her body. Since auditory hallucinations were the norm in this microcosm of patients, the members viewed her "little green men" as evidence of *real* craziness and appeared to adopt the same quizzical attitude toward her as most other people did toward them, underlining once again that normalcy is relative.

A Russian patient who had been in this country for about 20 years was in a five-day length of stay hospital detoxification unit. Group therapy was only available twice a week and while here he attended the only group therapy session for substance abusers that would be possible for him. It was important, therefore, to help him gain as much insight as possible during the allotted time.

He was asked what he did for a living and replied he helped take care of elderly people in their homes. In Russia, he had been a military officer and acknowledged he had served in Afghanistan. When gently asked if he had made 'errors' there, he nodded affirmatively. Someone in the group asked if he had killed innocent children and civilians. A pained expression crossed his face and he mumbled that was a private matter. His sadness was palpable.

When asked why he drank, he shrugged his shoulders and gave some vague explanation of how it helped him try to forget his terrible memories. Despite this attempt at self-medication, however, he continued to have what he described as painfully vivid dreams but would not discuss their content except to say the dreams often seemed very real.

As all this material rolled out, previously compartmentalized and suppressed but now interconnected for perhaps the first time, it didn't take much effort or explanation for him to see the related antecedents to his dreams and his drinking. He also began to recognize his dramatic loss of status upon arriving in this country as a basis for his depression.

At the end of the group, he expressed appreciation for the clarity and release this experience had given him. He agreed to attend support groups to stop drinking, and to seek regular individual psychotherapy after his discharge, in order to capitalize on this breakthrough. One can only hope for the best.

A young man in another psychotherapy group shared that his abusive experiences growing up in the housing projects had prepared him for the harsh realities of adulthood far better than the upbringing of any of the professionals in the room. After all, he surmised, they had been brought up in 'happily ever after' fairy tale homes, privileged and treated with kid gloves, only to eventually have to face the shock from which he had already been insulated. What an interesting twist on the optimal developmental environment.

Several students from various mental health disciplines were observing a group psychotherapy session. The patients were deep into a discussion concerning their anxieties and the depressive feelings related to growing older alone. The group members were very attentive and offered each other much empathy and support as they shared related experiences. Suddenly, a young female patient turned to me and matter-of-factly asked: "When was the last time you had a blow job?" This sent understandable shock waves through the group.

In an attempt to minimize the intensity of her comment, I supportively treated her question as a contribution to the discussion, noting she was describing another aspect of attempts at human closeness, the very subject at hand. Clearly the embarrassment the patient had hoped to induce in me did not materialize nor did any sort of moralistic reprimand result, a disappointment for the patient if her aim was negative attention. She didn't give up so easily, however. In the middle of my sentence she interjected: "You look like you need a blow job." Perhaps I might have expressed appreciation for her concern for my welfare, but instead I simply continued the theme of her unique focus on physical contact, reframing it in as positive a way as possible, again as if this was not an unusual topic for discussion. The group continued, more or less smoothly, to the conclusion that close human relationships were one antidote to loneliness and social isolation. The humorous aspect of this non-sensationally handled encounter actually left most group members in an upbeat mood.

While reviewing the group with the students later that day, they expressed apprehensiveness that such a question might someday be posed to them. I encouraged them to explore their own anxieties about so-called taboo subjects and advised them to be ready for anything when working in this field. If and when it happens, they should not take it personally. The central point I wanted to demonstrate for these students was that no matter how bizarre or deviant a patient's comments initially seem, it is often possible to extract something meaningful and applicable to the discussion at hand. Being able to accomplish this sustains the integrity of the discussion and, at the same time, supports the patients, assures them they are in a safe environment and minimizes the potential for alienation from the group. Additionally, the patients may be helped attain a clearer understanding of the meaning of what was said, possibly reducing some of the anxiety that often accompanies confused or inappropriate remarks.

During clinical treatment planning conferences on the inpatient unit, I would routinely report on each group therapy session. On one occasion, in order to see if anyone was actually paying attention, I said, "The group began with a discussion of distrust, anger and depression. . . . Then I let the patients speak."

It took them a moment!

Outpatient groups

When young men were being drafted into military service during the Vietnam War, a law student and his wife asked to meet with me. He was determined to avoid having to serve in that war so he had gotten a psychiatrist to attest to the fact that his wife was "pathologically dependent" on him and, therefore, he could not leave her. His strategy in designating his wife as the patient was based on his concern the Character and Fitness Committee of the State Bar Association might not look favorably on his application if there was a psychiatric exclusion anywhere in his record.

The draft board apparently accepted the psychiatrist's report but stipulated she needed to undergo psychotherapy, presumably to alleviate the difficulty and also to validate his draft deferment.

At her very first group session, this attractive and somewhat narcissistic woman had no trouble talking about herself and quickly became the center of attention. During her second session, she gave the group a detailed account of the extramarital affair she was currently having. Subsequently, she never returned.

Treatment verification was never requested by the draft board and later I learned her husband's gambit had failed and he had indeed been drafted.

Notes

1 Empathy in psychotherapy was defined as "sensitive and generous listening" by H. Kohut, a 20th-century intellectual, psychoanalyst, teacher and scholar. He felt it was essential to the success of psychotherapy (talk therapy). In his highly influential book *The Analysis of the Self*, University of Chicago Press, 1971, Reprint edition (October 1, 2009), Kohut established the 'industry standard' for the treatment of personality disorders.

2 J. S. Fraser, and A. D. Salovey, *Second-Order Change in Psychotherapy*, Amer Psychological Assn, 1st edition (January 1, 2007). A substantial body of evidence has shown that psychotherapy can ameliorate psychological distress. The authors posit that various approaches to treatment can be successful if the therapist's approach is an empathic one. In this work they refer to "The golden thread that unifies effective treatments".

3 G. E. Berrios, and R. Luque, Cotard's Delusion or Syndrome? *Comprehensive Psychiatry*, Vol. 36: 218–223, 1955. Described in 1800 by Cotard, there continues to be debate.

4 Anonymous.

5 Frederick Perls, and Peter Philipp. *From Planned Psychotherapy to Gestalt Therapy: Essays and Lectures – 1945 to 1965*. The Gestalt Journal Press (January 26, 2012).

6 *Diagnostic and Statistical Manual of Mental Disorders V*, code: 308.3, American Psychiatric Association, 2013.

7 An abortion performed because of the mother's physical or mental health, or to prevent the birth of a deformed child or of a child conceived as a result of rape or incest. (Dictionary.com)

8 I. D. Yalom, *Inpatient Group Psychotherapy*, New York, NY: Basic Books, 1983.

9 The principal secret intelligence service of the state of Israel. M. Bar-Zohar, and N. Mishal, *Mossad: The Great Operations of Israel's Secret Service*, Sun Lakes, AZ: The Robson Press, 2012.

Chapter 9

WWII Holocaust survivors

The concept of arbitrary and authoritarian imposition of power on defenseless human beings was given new meaning, on a scale never before imagined, by the Nazis. The unending pain of the survivors and their children is incalculable, the events very much alive in their memories to this day.

At the mental health center where I worked we treated many Holocaust survivors and/or their families. Ongoing discussions took place amongst the staff regarding the pros and cons of various treatment approaches. Eventually an outside psychologist, a presumed expert in the field, was brought in to conduct a seminar for us. Her approach turned out to be rigid and fascistic, almost an echo of the persecution itself. Her working principle was that despite the reluctance of survivors to speak of the horrors of their experience, they must be made to do so, in fact from the very outset of the treatment, in order for the therapy to be successful.

There were several survivors on the staff, and they were in attendance at this seminar. The expert attempted to coerce them into recalling and speaking of their experiences, something no one was prepared for or interested in doing at that time and in that place. One staff member was reduced to tears after being intimidated into describing, in some detail, her two years of sitting still in hiding in an attic in Hungary. None of us could discern any apparent value to this exercise.

I became the focus of this psychologist's approach when she turned to me and, without the benefit of any preliminary therapeutic alliance, told me that the "non-Jewish" name we had given to my newborn daughter was clearly an attempt to protect her from future anti-Semitic pogroms! Well, that and the anti-tank gun in my basement!

The seminar was soon brought to an end, and we all agreed it was more about recapitulation than rehabilitation.

On an otherwise unremarkable summer evening at the mental health center we received an urgent call from the mother of one of our patients. (Both she and her husband were survivors of Nazi persecution before and during WWII.) Her son Joey (not his real name), a chronically psychotic man in his mid-30s, was presently terrorizing his family. Joey was well known to us on the day treatment service and had a history of assaultive behavior toward his parents.

As soon as this call came in, we immediately contacted the local police precinct. Two uniformed officers picked me up and I rode with them in a patrol car to Joey's house. One of the officers had been involved in a previous altercation with Joey during which Joey's skull had been fractured. The officer was now somewhat apprehensive as he had taken heat from his superiors because of the head injury. Given the anticipated stress of the upcoming confrontation and the fact that any anxiety was likely to be contagious and would easily escalate, I hoped my presence would reduce the likelihood of a major scuffle. Sustained reassurance and support can never be overdone.

Arriving in front of Joey's apartment building, I saw that a crowd had formed. We entered the hallway and I led the way to his second floor walk-up apartment, two armed and nervous cops behind me and a potentially assaultive, out of control mental patient in front. Ready for anything and hoping my skills would be equal to the situation within, I knocked on the door.

Joey's mother answered my knock and there at the kitchen table sat Joey, obviously relishing what looked like a delicious chicken dinner. Astonishingly, Joey's mother turned to us and asked, "Can Joey please finish his dinner before you take him away?" This was cognitive dissonance given new meaning, so far from what we had expected to encounter! I recovered quickly from my surprise, perhaps even feeling a little disappointed at the absence of any drama. With police concurrence I insisted that Joey had to come with us right now. Anticipating a confrontation but counting on my positive prior relationship with him, I explained it would be in his best interest if he came with us now, and I would consider it a personal favor to me if he did so.

Aware of the police presence, Joey agreed but was then informed that handcuffing was required, another potential provocation. Fortunately Joey did not object. In a gesture of support I stayed close by his side while he was cuffed, and then indicated to the family that we were leaving. The less time Joey had to think about this alternative to his chicken dinner, in his now warm again family environment, the better. In retrospect, I'm surprised his mother did not invite us all to sit down and share that delectable chicken!

We quickly exited the apartment with me in the lead, followed by one officer in front of Joey and one behind him. Outside the building the crowd was rather large yet oddly quiet, as if they sensed the sadness of this incident. Many of them apparently knew Joey and perhaps had seen this happen before.

We climbed into the police car, one officer behind the wheel and Joey in the back seat between the other officer and me. As we made our way through the streets to the hospital, Joey began to complain that the cuffs were too tight. Insisting they were on correctly, the officers evinced some anxiety. The one driving must have decided the less time spent with this patient the better so he turned on the turret lights and the siren and doubled his speed. Careening along the street I could see the light bouncing off buildings on either side. As we approached a stop sign, judging by our speed, it was apparent the driver had no intention of even slowing down. Just then, out of nowhere, a couple on a motor scooter appeared right in front of us, forcing our driver to brake and veer around them. How we managed to avoid running these two people over remains a mystery to me.

Arriving safely at the emergency department, the officers took their leave. Joey was all smiles now and seemed to need no further reassurance or comforting from me. Grinning, he told me he hadn't had such a good time in years!

There is a tragic backstory here: The time Joey actually *had* assaulted his parents, they were at first unable to bring themselves to call the police on their own child, no matter the danger to themselves. Once at the hospital, Joey's father had suddenly and unexpectedly described to me, in exquisite detail, how in WWII he had played dead on a field while the Germans raked it with machine gun fire. Joey carried the angst of his parent's unimaginable trauma.

Another Holocaust survivor I treated at the mental health center insisted the hospital maintain his records under a pseudonym. During WWII he had hidden the fact he was a Jew in order to avoid persecution and probably death. By posing as a Muslim, and working as secretary to a Nazi party official in Berlin, he had likely saved himself. It was almost 30 years after the end of the war when I first met this man yet he continued to exhibit symptoms of PTSD, including vivid, recurrent nightmares. Recently he had come to the conclusion he was entitled to reparations and he asked me to write a letter to the German authorities on his behalf. Rather than using my hospital stationery (which had the Star of David embossed on its letterhead), I instead chose to use my own, highlighting my Teutonic last name. I felt the Germans might be more responsive to that.

Gradually psychiatric treatment helped this patient recover from the pain of his terrible ordeal during WWII. The reparations eventually awarded to him by the German government reflected their acknowledgement of the injustice done to him and afforded him not only a sense of closure, but an improved income as well.

A personal friend since our college days had finally become aware of how much he had been traumatized as a child in a Nazi concentration camp and during his subsequent liberation to a Displaced Persons Camp. After deciding to file a claim for reparations from the German government, he asked me to perform a psychological examination to support his claim. The results of my evaluation clearly corroborated his assertion of substantial and lasting distress.

We agreed to meet in a neighborhood pub so I could give him the written report to submit to the German authorities. As we were reviewing my findings, he suddenly remembered I was also supposed to have treated him. So, I did! I paid for his drink!

On an even more personal level, my mother-in-law had been receiving monthly reparation payments from the German government for the murder of her parents and the confiscation of their personal and business properties. They were German citizens living in Berlin at the time of the Holocaust.

A little less than a year after she died, my wife and her sister received letters from the Bundesversicherungsanstalt fur Angestellte (loosely translated as the Federal Pension Accounting Agency) informing them they owed the German government money for a check cashed after their mother's death. "*Die fur Zeit nach dem Sterbemonat des Rentenberechtigten gezahlten Rentbetrage sind uberzahlt,*" they said! ("The pension amounts paid after the month of death constitute an overpayment.") This from the country that confiscated all of my mother-in-law's assets before the war! They demanded restitution of DM 1,552,08, approximately $1,500 USD at the time.

The initial demand was written in German (which neither I nor my wife speak), and required considerable effort to translate. Once that was accomplished, my wife responded that she had not cashed any checks, nor had her sister, adding: "If, as you claim, a payment (was paid) after my mother's death . . . you must furnish me with a copy of this cancelled check showing the endorsement on the back." The Bundesversicherungsanstalt fur Angestellte never complied. They did, however, continue to send progressively more threatening letters, mostly in English now. Again, this from the country that looted all of Europe! The final letter, received about a year and a half after the first one, was from the Vice Consul representing the Generalkonsulat der Bundesrepublik Deutschland (Consulate General of the Federal Republic of Germany). It stated, again in English lest we miss the point, "Should you fail to comply with this last notice to pay . . . be assured that I will not hesitate to recommend strongly legal action to be taken against you with the local US court of jurisdiction."

So, before the 'SS'[1] could come to our home and kick in our door, I called the Vice Consul at the Consulate General in New York and referenced her last threatening letter. The Vice Consul could not explain their failure to send us a copy of a cancelled check. I informed her that this continuing harassment and re-victimization of our family was evoking very painful memories. I repeated that we had not taken the money and pointed out that these reparations were but a minuscule amount considering the suffering and loss of life and property that had been imposed on my mother-in-law's family, and that it seemed quite insensitive of the German government, considering their history, to be making such an issue over such a paltry sum given the context of its origin. The Vice Consul quickly corrected me: "These payments were actually 'social security', not reparations" reminding me of a Mel Brooks line in his 'Nuremberg Film Festival'[2] routine: "After all, what was it all about? Sent some people to camp; mostly in the summer!"

Before hanging up, I told the Vice Consul that my family was not going to tolerate this continued harassment and that if I heard from her or her aSSociates again, I would take the matter to the State Department and *The New York Post*. Apparently that ended the matter. Probably it was the threat of *The New York Post* that did it!

Given these un-menschen-able[3] historical accounts, it would certainly be a 'shanda'* to go to Europe and 'not see'** Germany!

Notes

1 SS, abbreviation of Schutzstaffel (German: "Protective Echelon"), the black-uniformed elite corps and self-described "political soldiers" of the Nazi Party. Encyclopaedia Britannica.
2 2000 Years with Carl Reiner & Mel Brooks, Brooksfilms Ltd. & ClearProductions Inc., Rhino Records Inc. 1994.
3 Derived from the word "mensch", Yiddish for 'human being', a person of honor and integrity.

* Yiddish for 'shame'.
** 'not see' = Nazi.

Chapter 10

Testifying in court

Mental health professionals are often called upon to perform psychological evaluations, and submit written reports, for patients involved in legal action. Occasionally we are also asked to provide oral testimony in court.

The New York City law department once referred a case to me where a pedestrian had been struck by a police car during a parade. The city was trying to prove the man's current cognitive deficits were the result of a pre-existing condition and not of the accident. My examination found that his deficits were likely the direct result of head trauma sustained in the accident. This finding was supported by several other examiners as well.

More than 15 years later I was asked to testify for this same patient at a hearing, not for the *still-pending* multimillion-dollar lawsuit against the city, but because he had declared bankruptcy at some point and his lawyer had neglected to list his potential gain from the accident as a future asset. The hearing now was to determine whether the man had the cognitive capacity to knowingly participate in a conspiracy to hide that asset. I was given a copy of my original report and asked to confirm that the man remained too impaired to have knowingly participated in any kind of fraud.

Upon completion of my testimony the judge asked me to explain the term "vegetative depression," a severe disabling form of depression that I had ruled out in my report. I considered saying it's the kind of depression vegetarians get but thought better of it and dutifully explained the clinical meaning, thereby avoiding any possibility of a contempt citation.

Several months later, the judge handed down her decision that this man did not have the capacity to intentionally deceive and thus there was no bad faith with respect to his bankruptcy proceeding. He was allowed to resume his lawsuit and eventually it was settled out of court. The resolution was so long in coming, however, that despite the plaintiff's eventual success, "Justice delayed . . ."[1] still applied here.

Another time I was asked by an attorney to examine an adolescent Hispanic boy who had sustained a broken arm while on vacation in Puerto Rico. The arm was casted at a local hospital in Puerto Rico, but soon after his arrival back on the mainland, the boy began complaining of significant pain and discomfort in the affected arm. His parents took him to a city hospital where they were told there was nothing wrong. The boy's complaints, however, continued to escalate and eventually he was taken to a different hospital for second opinion. The doctors at this facility removed the cast and found substantial gangrene necessitating amputation. Alleging negligence and malpractice resulting in amputation, with significant subsequent loss of productivity and potential earnings, the attorney wanted me to provide written documentation of the boy's above-average intelligence to support my testimony in the lawsuit against the first city hospital. My findings supported the plaintiff.

The case went to trial at a time when there was a great deal of publicity and political agitation over excessive damages awarded in malpractice suits. The jury, comprised solely of white men, found for the defendant and further concluded it was the hospital in Puerto Rico that was the negligent party. While we can't be certain of the extent to which the jury was influenced by the politics of the day, once again . . . "Justice denied . . ."

Note

1 W. Gladstone. "Justice delayed is justice denied." Address to Parliament on the adoption of the disestablishment of the Church of Ireland as a policy of the Liberal Party, on 16 March 1868.

Chapter 11

Screening of police applicants

Applicants disqualified by the NYPD Police Academy, after an initial evaluation, are offered the opportunity to obtain a second opinion from an outside psychologist. I recall four such applicants referred to me over the years and, in each case, I concurred with the original decision of the police department.

One was a female who primarily saw vaginas on the Rorschach Ink-blot test, with very unusual frequency and, after each card was shown, she would point down to her own.

Another was a male applicant who carried a gun (allegedly licensed) to my office because he felt my relatively peaceful neighborhood was "dangerous".

The third was a man who agreed with this statement on the Cornell Medical Index:[1] "I have strange and peculiar thoughts." He was disqualified, not because he had such thoughts, as most of us do at one time or another, but because he didn't have the good judgment to keep it to himself, as most of us would.

Last was a man who had received a medical discharge from the US Army because he refused to touch any weapons. He could not explain how he would get around the requirement, as a police officer, to carry and use a weapon.

Note

1 Developed in 1949, this self-administered tool is used to collect information about a person's health status. (www.webmedcentral.com/article_view/909)

Chapter 12

Clinicians in harm's way

There is ample documentation in the literature that a significant number of mental health practitioners have been threatened with, or actually physically assaulted by patients at some point in their careers.[1, 2] Here are two personal experiences:

An agitated female inpatient, one I had treated for a long time in and out of the hospital, was being forcibly restrained by two NYPD officers who had just brought her to the unit. Foolishly assuming she would recognize and trust me because of our ongoing relationship, I approached her to offer support and help calm her down. The well-placed kick she landed on my groin was totally unexpected, and my daughter probably owes her existence to the fact that the patient was wearing sneakers at the time.

In the second example, a woman I had been treating as an outpatient demanded to be admitted to the inpatient unit. Given her chronic personality issues, some of which had made her resistant to discharge in the past, it was my professional judgment that she would not benefit from hospitalization. The patient became so angry and frustrated with my opposition to her demand that she threw a cup of hot water at me when I momentarily turned my back. There was surprise and pain but, fortunately, no serious injury. Hospital policy at that time discouraged staff from filing police complaints against patients in all but the most serious offenses, as a matter of maintaining treatment confidentiality, not to mention covering the hospital's ass. CYA again!

To add insult to my injury, and over my continuing objections, the patient was nevertheless admitted to the inpatient unit. Having had my treatment alliance with her disrupted by the admission, I suggested the psychiatrist who had admitted her take the case going forward, which he did. There was no improvement in her negative behavior and every time they tried to discharge her, she found a way to stay, once even going so far as to put her fist through a glass partition.

As well as these actual physical assaults, there have also been incidents where I was threatened, or the potential for harm was very real.

The patient just mentioned above once filed a complaint against me with the state professional disciplinary board alleging I had violated her confidentiality when I advocated, on her behalf, for the community advisory board of the mental health center to allow her to speak about patients' concerns. Although this was done at her request, and although she was already known by name to the entire committee, she nevertheless insisted that somehow her confidentiality had been violated. The state was obligated to investigate the complaint and subsequently found it to be without merit. This only further exacerbated the patient's resentment toward me. She subsequently threatened me with violence, however, there were no further attacks, and I have since learned she died.

Another woman I was treating at the hospital, on an outpatient basis, worked at a state facility for the developmentally disabled where she had recently brought a Workers Compensation case against an armed security guard for alleged stalking and sexual harassment. Despite the case against him, the stalking persisted and eventually resulted in her taking additional legal action.

After a civil court subpoenaed my records for this patient, I had some concern this exposed me to possible retribution from the security guard; however, nothing ever came of this and I never learned of the outcome.

Then there was the public official I treated who was involved in a criminal investigation focused on an allegation that he had paid a bribe to organized crime figures for his rather important position. The investigation was terminated a short while later, and charges were never filed. Nevertheless, it did cross my mind that I might be sought out by those crime figures as having information compromising to their interests by virtue of my confidential relationship with this patient. Fortunately, life proceeded without incident.

A woman recently discharged from inpatient care persisted in calling me at the hospital and at my home, despite my considerable efforts to discourage her. On several occasions her verbalizations on the phone alternated between suicidal and homicidal threats. She frequently expressed a romantic interest in me and jealousy of my family, even threatening to harm my wife. She actually showed up at my home once, yelling and banging on the front door. After a brief supportive discussion outside my residence, she agreed to leave but the assaultive potential was real.

Reluctantly, but prudently, this time I filed a police report. Although the patient continued to be treated at the hospital, she never turned up at my door again.

After a series of inappropriate and unprofessional remarks to patients and supervisors, a psychiatric resident was terminated from the hospital's residency training program. He was also arrested around this time and convicted of possessing hollow point bullets. My involvement in the decision to dismiss him from our program caused me some anxiety he might attempt to retaliate. The fact that the police never found a gun only compounded my unease.

A male patient with an antisocial personality disorder, and a prior conviction for rape, was being treated in our day treatment service. Frequently he made threatening remarks toward staff and their families, but at other times he could be friendly and even charming.

Several years after he was discharged, I ran into him on the inpatient unit of another hospital where I was consulting. In the intervening time he had again been in prison and now seemed far more passive, perhaps worn down by the system. Greeting me as warmly as if we had been close friends, he alluded to all the 'great times' we shared in our mutual past but made no mention of his previous threats and menacing behaviors. One could almost imagine him saying something like: "Hey, remember those great intimidating threats I made toward all you guys in the old days?"

Aah . . . nostalgia!

At the time I was director of the inpatient unit, the professional staff, particularly the leadership, customarily played a major role if it became necessary to physically restrain a patient. Presumably this policy was intended to minimize the potential for provocativeness and insensitivity on the part of the professional staff as they, and not some hefty mental health worker, would realize the consequences if something went wrong.

How well I recall the day an unpredictable, clearly angry and dangerous young Hispanic male was in the intensive observation area. (Oddly, although it was referred to as the "Blue Room", it had long ago been painted a cognitively dissonant shade of white.) Jose (not the patient's real name) had just destroyed a piece of furniture and was holding a long section of drawer over his shoulder, like a baseball bat, threatening to harm someone. As the clinician in charge, I was called to handle the situation. There I stood, less than ten feet in front of Jose, who had his back to the window. Two staff members stood behind me and off to one side while the rest of the staff maintained a discreet distance. Their impatience with the situation was palpable.

As Jose stared at me I looked back at him with what I hoped was a friendly expression. Jose didn't speak a word of English, and I didn't speak a word of Spanish. Quietly, I asked for an interpreter and eventually one arrived. We asked the patient about his concerns. He was unclear why he was feeling so angry and aggressive, so I attempted to engage him in a dialogue. Surprised that under these circumstances someone wanted to have a calm, rational conversation with him, he relaxed slightly. Nevertheless, I was not unaware of the potential for precipitous interventions from the uneasy staff behind me. Apparently in need of some form of immediate tension release, they were on the verge of provoking a premature and unnecessary free-for-all where injury to someone was guaranteed.

As the tension mounted, I continued talking with the patient, motioning for the staff to stay back. I was developing an alliance with Jose, while mine with the fulminating, aggressive staff behind me was diminishing. Finally, a nurse standing safely toward the rear of the room, in a soft but firm voice urged: "*Take him now!*" (It reminded me of the old Westerns where, under similar circumstances, someone would shout, "Somebody get a rope!")

"*You* take him now!" I said, the sarcasm in my voice unmistakable as I gestured they were not to approach. My authority held.

After a full 45 minutes I was able to talk Jose not only into peacefully giving up his weapon, but also to being placed in restraints. Ironically, no one seemed to regard this outcome with the awe and admiration it deserved. Although tensions smoldered, gradually there was an uneasy but quiet return to normal duties.

Later that afternoon a brief but telling incident took place. A bright, likeable Hispanic patient who had been out on a pass, returned to the unit hiding a can of beer under his arm. He had no history of violent acting-out and, in fact, he was probably too self-effacing for his own good. Of course, it was necessary to take the beer away from him, so I said to him, in a friendly manner, "Well, I guess you're going to be "sadder Budweiser!" He smiled in acknowledgment of my humorous, non-authoritarian remark and took a step toward me intending to hand over the can. The staff, misinterpreting this action, jumped to the conclusion he was about to assault me ("The fear is the wish."),[3] and pounced on him. Bizarrely, however, they picked up both of us as one entity and threw us onto a bed already prepared with full restraints. Before anyone realized what was happening, my leg was put in a leather restraint. At least four people piled on top of me, a form of intimacy I must confess I fear. The ridiculousness of the scene was sufficient to elicit laughter from patients and staff alike, finally diffusing the tensions of the day for everyone.

Another potentially dangerous situation occurred when we needed to convert a psychotic inpatient to involuntary status after he suddenly became more likely to harm himself. This included the possibility we would have to forcibly restrain him to prevent him from leaving the hospital. It was my responsibility to convince this young man, with whom I previously had a positive relationship, that it was in everyone's best interests for him to consent to stay.

He agreed to meet alone with me in my office. The staff was poised outside my door, restraints at the ready, their adrenaline rising. I carefully explained the situation to the patient, but it soon became obvious he was not interested in cooperating.

"Look," I finally said to him. "There's no way you're going to get out of here, but how would you like to do me a favor and then I'd owe you one. The staff would be very impressed with both of us if you agree to stay and we would avoid a major brawl. If you sign the form, we won't have to restrain you and we'll both look good; you avoid a hassle and I'll owe you a favor."

The social leveling effect of giving him the option to 'make a deal' with me, along with the sense of some control this afforded him, helped reduce his anxiety and suspiciousness and enabled him to voluntarily agree to stay in the hospital.

It's all about the relationship.

Then there was the day a male social worker and I were in a small interview room on the inpatient unit talking to an angry patient who was threatening to hit someone. The patient was substantially larger than either of us, and obviously physically fit. The entire unit was aware of the situation and one could almost feel their eyes on us through the walls of the room. Four security guards were stationed around the corner, eagerly and impatiently awaiting the signal to "engage" the patient. The director of the unit was monitoring the situation from a secure location, behind glass doors, at the far end of the floor.

Previously, the social worker and I had developed a good relationship with this patient; as men, we all understood each other and he was not upset with us. He was irate by what he felt was the condescending and patronizing way the staff nurses (read that as 'women') talked to him and ordered him around.

"Why do they treat me like I'm a child?" he angrily asked. Good question! I could have cited the literature describing the behavioral effects on staff who operated within authoritarian, hierarchical organizations with stratified mobility, but somehow I didn't think it would have had a calming effect at that point. In fact, had I pondered that material too much at that moment, I might have sided with the patient. Instead, the social worker and I commiserated with him as best we could, drawing on our own comparable experiences. As we talked and played for time, we formed a male alliance and, while still not ready to comply with our request for voluntary acceptance of physical restraints (an immutable decision made by the director), the patient had begun to relax a little and it appeared that our strategy of giving him as much time as he needed to calm down, so as to avoid serious bloodshed (likely ours), was working.

Just then the door creaked open, a distraction our brittle situation did not need at that moment. A staff member entered, gingerly handed over a note from the director and then quickly retreated. The patient and the social worker both looked quizzically on as I read the note.

"Take him now!" it said. (Yes, it really did!) This was the message from the man behind glass doors, 50 yards away, with four security guards between him and us. In my judgment there was no way I could, or even needed to "take him now", without grave, unnecessary consequences. I had no doubt, then or now, that any attempt on my part to "take him now", or even to call for the security guards would have resulted in serious injury to all three of us. I decided to continue with our strategy, even as the grumblings of irritable nurses became increasingly audible through the closed door.

Recognizing the note had probably added to the patient's already substantial paranoid anxiety, I decided to tell him who it was from and what it said. When I finished reading, he looked at the social worker and me, two physically unimpressive men compared to him, and the three of us broke into spontaneous prolonged laughter. The utter ludicrousness of the order was not lost on him.

I believe the patient's decision, 20 or so minutes later, to voluntarily go into restraints, was a gesture of support for his true buddies on the unit, the social worker and me. This probably disappointed security and certainly made the director's impatience and distancing seem foolish, perhaps even cowardly. Is it possible the director had brilliantly contrived his note to that end? Unlikely. The nurses whose attitudes had precipitated the incident seemed equally disappointed that the patient wasn't dealt with in a more punitive manner, but they did manage to contain themselves as, after all, they were trained professionals. (Weren't they?)

Lastly, I can recall the inpatient who was serially assaulting staff members. The director counseled patience and understanding, up until the time the patient punched him, whereupon he immediately had the patient sent to a state hospital.

Notes

1 https://kspope.com/stalking.php.
2 H. A. Bernstein, Survey of Threats and Assaults Directed toward Psycho-therapists. *American Journal of Psychotherapy*, Vol. 35, No. 4, 542–549, October 1981.
3 S. Freud, *The Interpretation of Dreams* (1900). New York, NY: Basic Books, 1st edition (February 23, 2010).

Chapter 13

Curious and troublesome clinical experiences

Treating behavioral disorders often involves conflicting expectations, contradictory assessments and unexpected outcomes. Elements of tragedy and comedy often confound attempts to sustain clinical objectivity. The experiences can be difficult, unpredictable, sometimes draining and often fulfilling, but never uninteresting for the clinician.

A rather complicated case was to be presented at our department's Grand Rounds. The patient's history included developmental disabilities as well as brain trauma from an assault; she was now in the early stages of a serious degenerative neurological disorder. In preparation for the presentation, one of our psychiatrists conducted a videotaped examination that was subsequently viewed by the staff. The patient's cognitive deficits (impaired memory and disorganized thinking) were clearly evident during the examination, and she often resorted to confabulation to compensate for her impaired long- and short-term memory. When she claimed to have gone to college, the psychiatrist asked if she had graduated. With great dignity and formality, as well the air of certainty that often accompanies confabulation, she answered she had graduated "*Suma Cuma Luca*".[1]

To his credit, the psychiatrist managed to retain his composure during the interview, while the less experienced staff among us broke out in unrestrained laughter as they viewed the video and reacted to what was perhaps their first exposure to the dissonance of a neologism born in a clinical context.

An emotionally difficult case involved a floridly psychotic, very obviously pregnant young woman who presented to the emergency department whereupon she immediately gave birth. After the delivery, when shown her newborn baby, she denied it was hers and steadfastly adhered to the delusion that she had been "hit by a truck". She clung to this extreme form of denial even after subsequent psychiatric hospitalization and treatment.

Once discharged to outpatient care, she continued to repudiate the fact she had given birth and rejected any relationship with the baby. I don't recall, perhaps as a product of my own denial over the sadness of the situation, the ultimate fate of the infant.

In a Treatment Planning Conference one day, we discussed a patient who was evasive about her history. We had previously learned she was studying to be a chef at a *culin*ary institute and hoped that if we could find out which school she was attending, we might have a link to locating her family and finding out more about her.

Despite our best efforts, the patient could not provide any further information so I recommended she be administered a '*culin*-oscopy'!

At another treatment planning meeting, a case manager presented a patient with elevated mood and continuous rapid, pressured speech. She reported the patient kept demanding gum to chew, raising the question of where all this gum was going as well as the logistics of obtaining sufficient supplies to meet her demand.

Some staff members suggested she be put on a schedule to control the amount of gum chewing but others characterized this plan as infantilizing. The resulting 'clinical' conflict led to an unnecessarily prolonged and useless discussion that came to an abrupt end when I pointed out that, like the current national debate, we seemed to be divided on 'gum control'!

One morning a female inpatient reported she had swallowed a number of staples ("That Was Easy"),[2] and explained how she had pried them off the back of a chair in her room. The nursing staff immediately decided the 60-plus chairs on the unit were unsafe and quickly had them removed from the inpatient units, without benefit of discussion with the rest of the clinical or administrative staff, not even the inpatient director. X-rays subsequently confirmed the patient had indeed swallowed the staples.

This nursing staff's maneuver served to enhance the patient's sense of power stemming from her narcissistic personality disorder, in part the very problem for which she had been hospitalized. It was also likely this created an incentive for her to escalate her behavior to possibly even more dangerous levels. Undoubtedly there were other ways the safety issue might have been dealt with.

The patient was also pleased to learn the X-rays revealed the presence of constipation with a fecal impaction, a condition she said she had been complaining about for some time without adequate treatment. In this way, the patient's seemingly random borderline[3] act might actually have served to draw attention to her previously untreated medical disorder.

One might conclude, therefore, that causing the staff to have this 'moving' experience (the chairs) was possibly in the interest of the patient finally having a 'moving' experience herself!

Then there was the 'sobering' experience with an outpatient who suffered from depression and severe alcoholism. One day he phoned from his home saying he was going into "DTs"[4] and needed immediate help. I called for an ambulance but then decided to drive to his house myself, arriving well before the ambulance. I was already helping the patient down the stairs when the paramedics arrived and together we assisted him into the ambulance.

At the ER, treatment was immediately initiated and once the patient was stabilized, the resident turned to me and asked, "Why don't you just kill him?" From the resident's point of view this man's 'irresponsible' behavior was causing needless expense and wasting an excessive amount of medical personnel time. I tried to explain that the patient's behavior was beyond his volitional control, but this only resulted in the resident contemptuously commenting on my naiveté.

Sadly, it is not unusual for health-care professionals to dehumanize patients, often as a means of protecting themselves from the pain they witness and the feelings of anger and inadequacy they experience in response to self-destructive behaviors.

Another of our patients was a woman with chronically impaired judgment. Because of a medical condition, she had been cautioned not to drink alcohol or ingest dairy products, and warned that serious adverse physical consequences could result.

Despite our best efforts she continued to consume both, and the staff was very frustrated with her. I sardonically suggested that perhaps the patient could save herself a lot of time by simply drinking Bailey's Irish Cream!

A colleague once related a case involving a woman who presented to the emergency department with a chief complaint of "worms coming out of her arm". During the initial interview by the intake nurse, the patient rubbed her arm vigorously and said, "See the worms? My son also sees them."

The nurse then went out to the hall to interview the son who had accompanied his mother to the hospital. Acknowledging he had the same problem, he rubbed his arm and held it out for inspection. Obviously there were no worms coming out of their arms, and the nurse concluded this was a shared psychosis. Mother and son were both admitted to our psychiatric inpatient unit.

A manic physician-gone-berserk was hospitalized on our inpatient unit and confined to a seclusion room. He somehow managed to jump out of the 'secure unbreakable' window in that room, four stories up, landing on top of a car parked illegally behind the mental health center. Sustaining only minimal injuries, he kept going until the staff finally caught up to him climbing over the back fence.

The improperly parked car he'd landed on belonged to a security guard. This raised certain interesting questions: Did the fact that the presence of the car might have saved the life of this patient put this employee in a good light with his supervisors? Or, given the fact that a lawsuit was going to be filed concerning the injuries sustained by the patient, would his death have been less expensive for the hospital?

While the guard apparently did not get into any serious trouble, one might say, given the unique circumstances here, that he probably should have carried "No Fall" insurance.

During another of our treatment planning conferences, a senior staff psychiatrist quietly came into the room. At a pause in the discussion, he mused about recent local atrocities: Homeless men were being set on fire in a run-down section of the city. He asked us to speculate on the possible diagnosis of someone who would commit this kind of crime.

"Republican," I suggested!

On an otherwise ordinary day, two local policemen were leaving a luncheonette near the hospital, their take-out food in hand, when they came upon three armed men who had just robbed an attorney's office next door. The perpetrators were dressed in traditional Hasidic[5] garb, which momentarily confused the officers as the hospital is in an Orthodox Jewish neighborhood. However, quickly reacting to the sight of their weapons, the police engaged them in a round of gunfire. One cop was wounded, two of the culprits were apprehended, and the third escaped toward the hospital.

A vanguard of police, including the requisite helicopter, quickly appeared on the scene; the commotion was earsplitting. Assuming the fugitive had entered the hospital, the police cordoned off the entire area and began a search. Rumors were flying (along with the helicopter) as to the whereabouts of the escaped robber.

On the day treatment service floor at that time were many seriously ill psychiatric patients, some actively engaged in therapy and others either pre- or post-treatment. In the midst of this, two policemen, now disguised as doctors in white coats, came on the floor. They moved on in the direction of the adjoining outpatient obstetrics and gynecology (OB-GYN) clinic. "Police?" one staff member asked them. They nodded in the affirmative, not appearing happy about the fact they had been 'made'. They shuffled off through the fire door in the direction of the OB-GYN clinic looking very much like the Marx Brothers.[6]

A few minutes later the elevator doors opened and a SWAT team of helmeted men with grim faces, Kevlar vests and shotguns spilled out onto the floor.

Concerned for the welfare of our patients, I cautioned them: "This is a psychiatric area with many fragile, sensitive and seriously ill patients." Their sergeant, assuming dangerous 'psychos' now surrounded him, gruffly but bravely responded: "If everyone stays calm, nobody will get hurt!" He then asked us where the "white-coated doctors" had gone. We pointed toward the OB-GYN clinic and they disappeared through the fire doors, single-file in the style of the Seven Dwarves.[7]

A few minutes later, applause was heard from the street. Glancing out of the window, we could see policemen shaking hands with each other. The fugitive had been safely captured in the waiting area of the OB-GYN clinic where he foolishly had tried to blend in as a patient, not realizing that men, with or without false beards, were not treated in there.

Just before Thanksgiving one year, I was standing in the hallway of the mental health center conversing with a female African-American colleague. A senior psychiatrist joined us, and the conversation turned to the subject of roast turkey. With a leer, the psychiatrist remarked that he didn't "eat dark meat", and walked off with a smug and knowing look on his face. My African-American coworker and I were dumbfounded by the racial and sexual undertones of this remark, not to mention the complete lack of social sensitivity.

Several clinicians visiting from another agency were waiting to meet with me, the director of Day Treatment, in my office. As I entered, they were discussing exercise on their stationary bicycles. One person was saying she had a screen and DVD player on her bike and as she exercised, she could watch a video that simulated riding on a country road in Vermont. Everyone murmured approval and indicated they engaged in similar practices.

Deadpan, before even introducing myself, I shared my own, somewhat analogous experience. "I ride a real bike on a country road every weekend," I said. "I have a portable DVD player on my handlebars and I play a video of my living room. It's just like being on a stationary bike." What followed was a brief moment when I could see them trying to absorb the surreal nature of what I had just said.

Eventually they got it and we went on to have a polite, informal meeting but I'm not sure they believed I was actually the director.

In a cafeteria-style restaurant near the hospital, the overhead menu board listed both vegetable soup and pea soup. While waiting on line I observed that no matter which soup a customer requested, the servings were ladled from the same kettle. When it was my turn, I confronted the server with this apparent deception.

Amiably he replied, "Peas are vegetables!"

Notes

1 A distortion of Summa Cum Laude, the academic level of distinction used by educational institutions to signify an academic degree conferred "with highest honor".
2 With apologies to Staples™.
3 Borderline Personality Disorder. DSM V. Rev 2013.
4 Delirium tremens is an acute episode of delirium, confusion and even seizures that is usually caused by withdrawal from alcohol.
5 Referring to a branch of Orthodox Judaism where the men wear black clothing, beards and long, curled sideburns.
6 The Marx Brothers was a family comedy act, originally from New York City, that enjoyed success in vaudeville, on Broadway and in motion pictures from 1905 to 1949.
7 The Seven Dwarves, from the story of Snow White. They lived in a tiny cottage and worked in the nearby mines. Snow White, hiding in the woods, happened upon their house after being told by the Huntsman to flee from the wicked Queen's kingdom.

Chapter 14

Absurd staff behavior

Social workers

A social worker I worked with once formulated this incredible diagnostic impression of a patient: "He's hiding his pathology behind a façade of health." To some extent don't we all?

Following a case presentation of an Orthodox Jewish patient who supported her substantial drug addition by prostituting herself, one of our Orthodox Jewish social workers (perhaps experiencing post-Purim depression as this was just after the Jewish holiday) responded by saying, "Well, she must have been adopted."

On a locked unit, a male inpatient was frequently heard muttering incoherently. He was also known to wear clothing alternately reflecting Jewish and Muslim religions. During a staff meeting, a social worker commented quizzically, "I don't get it. What is that about?" I leaned forward and in a mock confidential tone said, "I think he's mentally ill!"

Another time, that same social worker gave elaborate discharge instructions to a patient fully expecting he would follow them exactly but, no surprise, he didn't. If the patient had been able to follow such a complex set of individualized directions, he probably wouldn't have needed to be in the hospital in the first place.

Then there was the occasion when I knocked on the door of a colleague's office and entered without waiting for his response. Before me was a man pointing a handgun. Quickly I retreated, but before I could even sound an alarm, my colleague came flying out of his office yelling, "MAN WITH A GUN!"

The gunman ran out right behind him and fled down the stairs. Alongside him ran the rest of the staff and patients, all of them justifiably terrified. One of our secretaries, running adjacent to the gunman without realizing who he was, warned him there was a man with a gun on the loose. Later we learned he had dumped the handgun into a trashcan upon exiting the office.

Psychiatrists

In a staff meeting subsequent to the above incident, a macho hunter-type psychiatrist, originally from the Midwest, excoriated the social worker for his "cowardice" in the face of what we had learned by then was "only" a pellet gun. Never mind that a pellet gun is still a dangerous weapon, and who could possibly have made that distinction in the heat of the moment?

This insensitivity alienated the psychiatrist from most of the other staff from that time forward.

During a clinical conference, a senior psychiatrist commented on the finding of a golden to greenish-brown colored ring in the periphery of a patient's cornea, confident this was far too arcane a finding for any of the other clinicians in the room to recognize. However, having once seen a case in the state hospital, I dramatically exclaimed, "Not Wilson's disease?"[1]

The surprise of being upended in his professional specialty ultimately leveled the intellectual playing field between us.

Another psychiatrist on our staff was affectionately nicknamed "Dr. Magoo" because he often seemed bewildered, at times even disoriented, except when he was actively engaged in practicing his profession.

At a time well before the ubiquitous cell phone, Dr. Magoo was issued a standard pager device, with auditory and vibratory signal options, so that he could be reached when out of his office. Given what was clearly a mechanically complex item to him, it was not surprising that soon there were complaints from staff that he was not responding to his pages. Searching the hospital one day, I found him standing in the hallway wearing his usual perplexed expression.

"People have been paging you," I said.

"There must be something wrong with this thing," he replied. "Every once in a while it starts to shake on my belt."

A quick and obviously belated tutorial clarified the mystery for him.

A young Hispanic male, in the process of medically transitioning to becoming a female, was employed in the environmental services (house-keeping) department of the hospital and assigned to the mental health center. One of our senior psychiatrists was overtly uncomfortable with the transgender concept and struggled to make sense of it all. Eventually he managed to find a way to relate to her in a courteous, respectful and even comfortable manner.

When the holiday season arrived that year, obviously pleased with his newly acquired tolerance, the psychiatrist greeted her with a heartfelt, traditional "Feliz Navidad!?" She looked over at him and indignantly said, "I'm Jewish!"

Caught up in the urgency of a very critical department-wide policy-making meeting, a psychiatrist once interrupted saying, "We cannot afford the luxury of facts. We must act now!"

Sounds familiar these days!

Then there was the psychiatrist known for his idiosyncratic and unpredictable style of relating to staff and patients. Once, when we were discussing a rather fragile young Chinese-American woman, without any sense of his political incorrectness, and to the raucous reaction of the staff, he commented there were "*chinks* in her ego structure".*

Psychologists

Many years ago we had a psychologist on staff who was known for sequestering himself in his office where he built elaborate models of ancient sailing ships rather than actually seeing patients. This behavior was of concern for many reasons, not the least of which was that the clinic income was based on fee for service. In other words, he generated no income for the center if he wasn't seeing patients.

During a particularly tense administrative meeting when our financial problems were being discussed, I couldn't help but comment, sarcastically of course, that one consequence of the declining economics of the hospital was that this psychologist had been reduced to making only rowboats.

Then there was the Grand Rounds conference where a psychologist presented a case study of a patient with fecal erotic preoccupations. The psychologist had chosen the name "John" for this patient, presumably at random. When I pointed out the obvious connection of the pseudonym "John" to the patient's presenting problem, he was somewhat embarrassed.

---

* An ethnic slur used against someone of Asian origin but also a legitimate English word.

Many years ago a psychologist I worked with complained bitterly about a social worker on his clinical team: "She intimidates me in the staff meetings," he said. "Her comments make me feel stupid. I just don't know how to deal with her."

The social worker in question was a rather 'zaftig'** woman with long black hair who exuded a mother-earth kind of sensuality that was probably the root of her real threat to him. Playfully I offered him this politically incorrect advice: "The next time you feel she is giving you a hard time in a staff meeting, you immediately respond by saying, 'With those legs you have the nerve to criticize me?'" He gasped, imagining the collective retribution of his very politically correct colleagues, and said he would never have the nerve to say such a thing.

The next day, however, he returned with an expression on his face that indicated he had experienced an epiphany. "It worked," he exclaimed. Taken somewhat aback, I replied, "I never seriously meant for you to actually say that." "No, no," he chuckled. "I just *thought* it and it changed everything for me! I'm no longer intimidated."

Had we inadvertently anticipated cognitive behavioral therapy? This was certainly 'evidence based'.

Notes

1 A genetic disorder in which copper accumulates in tissues; this manifests as neurological or psychiatric symptoms and liver disease. Dictionary of Eye Terminology, 3rd edition; Barbara Cassin, Sheila A.B. Solomon.
2 "Merry Christmas" in Spanish.

** Yiddish for having a full rounded figure; plump.

Chapter 15

Awkward moments

Sitting at my desk on the inpatient unit one day, concentrating on something or other, I suddenly became aware of a slight ssssing noise just inside my open door. Looking up I was startled to see a patient (male, of course) casually urinating against the wall as if it were simply a matter of routine. Had he imagined a urinal? What does one say here?

In fact, it was not at all unusual to see a trail of urine or feces on the floor of the inpatient unit. Although one eventually becomes inured to this experience, there was the day I witnessed a grizzled looking patient (male, of course) reach into the back of his pajama pants and come out with a handful of steaming feces which he then slammed onto the table, giving new meaning to the expression, "Don't shit where you eat!" This was too much even for me, so I immediately went into hiding in my office.

A sad and agitated homeless man, covered with lice, was admitted to our inpatient unit. It fell to the three male staff members on the unit that day to douse the patient from head to foot with an anti-lice lotion while the patient was, of necessity, naked and in four point restraints.

We were doing fine until we reached the patient's genital area. Two of us looked uncomfortably at each other. Recalling that our third colleague was gay, we looked at him imploringly and he graciously completed the de-lousing task.

During a union strike at the hospital, management was left to cover all maintenance functions in the building. Given my experience in home repairs, I became the plumber; my main duty in this capacity was plunging stopped-up toilets. My own observation had long been that toilets in the community mental health building frequently became blocked, but I am not aware of any research linking toilet clogs to behavioral dysfunction.

Plunging toilets is usually a relatively simple procedure where pushing the plunger forcefully down into the toilet, repeating this one or two times as needed, usually clears a blockage. However, I vividly recall a time when this didn't work despite numerous attempts. Turning to a nurse in attendance I said, "Gloves please! I have to go in." I then manually cleared the obstruction, taking the concept of 'hands on' to new 'depths'.

Many years ago, when alternative sexual life styles were not as socially acceptable nor as openly discussed as they are today, a young psychiatrist was called to the emergency department to consult on a case where a patient had presented with an onion in his rectum. After reviewing the patient's history, the now disconcerted psychiatrist asked to be excused for just a moment.

Stepping out into the hall, he uttered a loud, tension-reducing "ARGHHHH!" and then returned to continue his examination with utmost professionalism.

A male patient spoke about sexual difficulties he and his fiancé were experiencing due to her medical problems. He then related the "creative" solution he had discovered: With his laptop computer perched on his chest, he watched internet pornography while she performed fellatio on him.

"Stan," I said. "What are you thinking? It's a lap top, not a chest top!"

After he chuckled appreciatively, we went on to talk about more intimate measures they might employ during the period of time she underwent medical treatment for her condition.

A female resident I was supervising in psychotherapy presented a case where the patient repeatedly complained about her husband's demands for oral sex. Whenever the patient raised this concern, the resident found that she would immediately change the subject. She acknowledged the topic was personally threatening, and that prevented her from talking with the patient about this issue.

During supervision, the resident was able to explore her own attitudes towards sexuality and her marriage, as well as some basic sex education topics. Subsequently there was sufficient resolution of her rather intense personal problems and she was able to minimize her countertransferential[1] resistance to exploring the material offered by the patient.

Eventually this resident learned that the patient's husband was actually offering the patient oral sex and not demanding it for himself, a fact completely obscured by the resident's earlier avoidance of the subject.

Here's a 'joke' that was told at a clinical staff meeting to make a point about forbidden behaviors and feelings, as well as the futility of 'magical thinking':[2] A terminally ill woman was in the intensive care unit. Heartbroken, her husband told her she had been a wonderful wife and he offered her anything she wanted before her death.

"Well," she said, "We never had anal sex." Sad but eager to comply, he drew the curtain around her bed and it was fantastic for both of them!

This went on for several days before it was realized her condition was improving. The doctors were puzzled but eventually acknowledged that she was, in fact, cured. On the day she was to be discharged, her husband began weeping inconsolably.

"What's wrong, dear? Why are you crying? I'm healed." Between shaking sobs he said, "I could have saved mom!"

Notes

1   First described publicly by Sigmund Freud in 1910 in "The Future Prospects of Psycho-Analytic Therapy", countertransference is when a therapist transfers emotions to a person in therapy.
2   "Magical thinking . . . is defined as the belief that an object, action or circumstance not logically related to a course of events can influence its outcome." (www.scientificamerican.com/article/superstitions-can-make-you/)

Chapter 16

Practicing when out of the office

No documentation required!

At social gatherings when people discover I'm a mental health professional, it is not unusual for one or more of them to ask for advice or technical clarification of a mental health concern.

One night at a dinner party, the woman I was seated next to began to ask my opinion on how she should relate to her nephew, a young man she said had been diagnosed with "schizophrenia". As she described his behaviors, her husband, a fairly pompous man, grew increasingly uncomfortable with her personal revelations and strongly suggested that she drop the subject. It was clear she resented his attempt to control her conversation and, with a definite edge to her voice, insisted on pursuing her line of questioning. He persisted and she resisted, to the growing discomfiture of the assembled dinner guests. Just as it appeared a full-blown dispute between them was about to erupt, I offered that I also did marital counseling. That brought the conversation to an abrupt halt!

On occasion I have found it useful to fall back on my professional training to 'reframe' a condescending remark made in a social context. For example, one warm summer night I was at an outdoor concert with my family. As Brahms' First Symphony was being performed, my 2-year-old daughter began to cry but, having presciently seated us at the rear of the lawn, I simply swept her up in my arms and headed for an area farther back that was devoid of people.

As I passed, a wise guy quipped: "What's the matter, doesn't she like Brahms?" "No," I replied. "It's the interpretation that's upsetting her!"

A retiring internist was showing me around an office suite that encompassed a portion of the first floor of the house I was about to purchase. One room included a very large, ancient looking X-ray machine. I could only imagine the entire neighborhood had probably been irradiated each time he used it but he assured me there was lead in the adjoining walls.

He then asked me, a psychologist, if I wanted him to leave the X-ray machine. I quickly declined, explaining I didn't delve that deeply into the unconscious.

Later on, when we were renovating and removed the wall separating the office from the kitchen, we found there was no lead!

And speaking of clinical hardware that might affect the residential neighborhood, there was a local psychiatrist who administered outpatient ECT in his home office. We used to jest about the lights dimming during dinner.

Part III

A challenging system

Chapter 17

Mental health advocacy

Politics and its discontents

As a young man becoming aware of the contradictions and hypocrisy of the system I was about to spend the rest of my professional life in, I began to engage in some independent activism. I wrote numerous letters to *The New York Times* and other publications, as well as to local and national politicians. This one was to the Editor, *New York Times*, dated October 1, 1966:

> I can't help wondering whether New York City officials read The Times. I am struck by the strange paradox of reading your Sept. 29 news report of the terrible conditions and lack of adequate facilities and equipment State Senator Thaler found at Kings County Hospital, ostensibly as a function of insufficient funds. Then a few days later I read of plans to allocate a substantial portion of $5.7 million to the construction of a horse stable. In addition, the design for the structure is to be chosen on the basis of a contest involving a hundred-thousand-dollar prize.
>
> How can New York City, in good conscience, spend that kind of money making sure some horses have a comfortable and healthy place to sleep when it doesn't seem able to do as much for its people, in or out of hospitals?

Another letter I wrote was to the Editor of *Time* magazine dated April 8, 1966, under the heading "Question of Progress". The letter evoked recollections of an early 20th-century movement known as Eugenics that employed "research typically focused on showing that the unfit were that way because of inferior genes that were multiplying rapidly, and that it was extremely expensive for 'normals' to provide care to such 'defectives'".[1]

> Judge Heller, quoted in "Prisoners" [March 25], might be surprised to learn that those 'genuine sub-humans' he refers to are regular

humans. And his statement seems to imply that in the case of genuine sub-humans we are justified in maintaining institutions with few if any, facilities for genuine treatment and rehabilitation of the mentally ill. The judge's attitudes betrayed in remarks that at first sound like the product of an enlightened age, may indicate that we have not progressed so far in our conceptions of what constitutes mental illness as we like to think.

'The more things stay the same, the more they stay the same.'[2]

Over time I gradually came to see that narrow and dysfunctional political and regulatory policies were preventing psychologists (as well as other non-physician mental health practitioners) from providing the highest level of care. Affording these professionals greater independence and autonomy would undoubtedly result in vastly improved services to patients.

So it was that in the early 1980s a psychology licensing bill was proposed in an effort to partially rectify this situation. At that time I wrote a letter to a NYS assemblyman in support of that bill spelling out the 'turf' issues that were limiting our ability to provide the most comprehensive care to patients:

First and most important, is the charge that this bill would create a monopoly for psychologists. The reality is that a *medical* monopoly already exists. The majority of mental health services in this state are not delivered through private practice, but rather in *institutions* controlled by the *medical* profession. Since medical doctors currently assume ultimate medical-legal responsibility for all patients in institutions regardless of which kind of mental health professional actually treats them, these physicians also retain most policy and overall clinical management positions within the institution. Since medical doctors are trained, for the most part, to view all disorders, including behavioral, as a product of disease, the structure of most of our mental health institutions reflects this attitude and these institutions still resemble hospitals for the treatment of the medically ill in every way including architecture, administration, treatment philosophy and the relative lack of autonomy of those practitioners who are not medical doctors. This kind of institutional constriction severely limits the potential for all mental health practitioners to develop *genuinely* innovative treatment approaches and *major* alterations in the way services are delivered to the public. It only serves to perpetuate a pseudo-medical approach to behavioral disorder by medical doctors and those others who wish to imitate their jargon and style in the pursuit of their own interests and status. Since the Psychology Licensing Bill grants *independent legal status* to psychologists, making them fully responsible for their work in any setting, a first step in breaking the current legal monopoly held by medical doctors is being made. If psychologists can establish themselves as truly *independent* practitioners, then they will be in a position to influence institutional policy-making because they will have equal legal standing with medical doctors and thus equal decision-making power. Since psychologists have a different perspective by virtue of their extensive training in behavior, the net effect will be a broadening of possibilities for the services that will be delivered by mental health institutions in New York. In addition, this move should encourage other recognized mental health professions such as social work and nursing to take a similar step, thus reducing still further the uniquely disproportionate power held now by physicians in the field of mental health.

I don't recall ever receiving a response!

The bill did eventually become law, however, subsequent efforts to further advance the legal/regulatory status of psychologists as autonomous professionals and independent service providers have had limited success.

In 1988 I made the following argument in connection with a legislative hearing on psychologists' initiative to obtain admitting privileges in psychiatric units of NYS hospitals:

It may seem obvious to state that psychologists already have the right *not* to admit patients to hospitals. Paradoxically, however, the decision to *not* admit a patient has the potential for far greater uncertainty and mishap. One must constantly be alert, when doing treatment, for the presence of suicidal or homicidal risk, acutely psychotic behavior, agitation, confusional states, etc. Every time I treat a patient and rule out the presence of these kinds of behaviors and do not recommend inpatient admission, I am making that decision autonomously and independently and my New York State license allows me to do so. Conversely, if I cause a patient to be admitted, immediately and automatically other professionals on the inpatient unit review my judgment. I submit, therefore, that the non-admissions by psychologists thousands of times a day is the more weighty and independent clinical judgment. Hospital admission is almost always the safer and essentially the *less* independent choice.[3]

In that same hearing, one of the legislators asked a testifying chair of a prominent psychiatric department how often they admit a patient referred to them by a psychologist. "Almost always," he said, effecting a respectful egalitarian attitude toward his colleagues, the psychologists. The legislator came back with, "Well then, I guess they know what they are doing, don't they?" The chairman, taken aback by his own seemingly generous remark being turned on him, had no response, and the legislator had no further questions. But, to date no such privileges have been granted in New York State.

The impact of dysfunctional political and regulatory policies on psychiatric treatment was summed up quite well by Jay Neugeboren, a distinguished author and educator, writing about the mental illness of his brother, Robert. Neugeboren made the point that a key element in the recovery of institutionalized mental patients was "a relationship with a human being". He went on to note,

> In New York State, there are more than 60,000 individuals living with psychiatric disabilities. What does it matter if one medication is superior to another if 34,500 of these people have no safe place to live, and therefore no opportunities to work, no choice of treatments and no access to dedicated individuals who are being paid decent wages to work with them?[4]

In reaction to a cost saving proposal to eliminate psychologists from Medicaid reimbursement in New York State, I made another attempt at advocating for psychologists and their patients. This letter appeared in Letters to the Editor of *The New York Times*, January 27, 1995:

> Your statement that the elimination of clinical psychology can be justified because it "would cause relatively little grief" is short-sighted. It is unacceptable that patients treated by psychologists, most of whom have severe and chronic mental illnesses, be deprived of this essential service at a maximum reimbursement rate of only $36 per treatment session.
>
> To understand why, one need only look at the cost-effectiveness of such a move. Psychologists account for only a tiny fraction of total Medicaid costs ($1 million out of a $16 billion budget). A patient

forced to terminate treatment with a psychologist will have to be treated at a mental health clinic for $60 to $90 a session, be hospitalized for several hundred dollars a day, or simply drop out of treatment. Only this last and morally distasteful alternative appears to save money. However, lack of treatment is likely to result in even more costly outcomes, such as anti-social behavior, which will add to the economic burdens of the criminal justice system.

Removing psychologists from Medicaid certainly makes bad economic sense. What makes good sense, when one considers the cost-effectiveness of their treatment, is giving psychologists an incentive for even greater participation in Medicaid. Now there's a money saving idea!

Success at last! We have remained as Medicaid providers, but at the pre-existing low reimbursement rate!

In a speech at a NYS Psychology Association convention several years later I highlighted our priority to optimally serve the public:

Our goal has always been to influence public policy, and mental health policy in particular, to the ultimate benefit of the general public as well as to the often marginalized and stigmatized mental health consumer. Given the extensive training, cumulative experience and altruism characteristic of our profession, this is the moral imperative we are obliged to follow so that consumers of psychological services in our society can obtain the best possible services.[5]

'The more things stay the same, the more they stay the same.'

It wasn't a great surprise when Mayor de Blasio of New York City, in an attempt to solve a vexing political problem involving carriage horses on New York City streets recently said "he would direct millions of dollars in public funds to create a commercial stable from an existing building"[6] in Central Park. This at a time when most New York City hospitals, among other obvious priorities, once again remain chronically underfunded! So again, 'the more things stay the same, the more they stay the same'.

Despite all the logic and evidence presented to legislators and other public officials, significant legislative or regulatory advances have yet to be seen. Sadly, even the psychology professional associations appear to have become discouraged and to have lost interest in the problems and limitations placed on psychologists in clinics and hospitals. The disastrous consequence has been a decline in the availability of psychology staff positions and internships.

Notes

1 Time Magazine, New York City.
2 With apologies to Jean-Baptiste Alphonse Karr (1808–1890), a French critic, journalist and novelist.
3 M. Heinrich, *Coalition of Hospital and Institutional Psychologists – CHIP-Newsletter*, Brooklyn, NY, April, 1988.
4 J. Neugeboren, *Newsweek*, New York City, February 6, 2006.
5 M. Heinrich, Acceptance Speech for the Allen V. Williams Award, New York State Psychological Association, 2007.
6 M. M. Grynbaum, With Horse Deal, Mayor Addresses A Vow But Gets New Troubles. *The New York Times*, Vol. CLXV, No. 57, 116, January 19, 2016.

Chapter 18

The appeal of 'prescription privileges'

"If you can't beat 'em, join 'em!"

It turns out that rather than continuing to advocate for increased utilization of our unique and distinguishing skills, some psychologists have been working toward having prescription privileges included in their scope of practice. To date, psychologists in at least five states (Louisiana, New Mexico, Illinois, Idaho and Iowa) have been successful. It probably has not escaped their notice that some individual psychiatrists, and the American Psychiatric Association, have done very well career-wise and financially in their association with the pharmaceutical industry.[1]

From a social policy point of view, the concern should be: Do we actually want or need another large segment of the mental health provider community to descend into the 15-minute, 'take two tablets and call me in the morning'[2] approach to the treatment of mental illness? Being able to see four patients in an hour, with the attendant financial advantage, may make serious intensive psychotherapy even less available and would certainly be a detriment to optimal, comprehensive treatment. Wouldn't a more progressive public policy be for psychologists to devote their time and resources to advocating for enhanced availability and reimbursement for the psychotherapies already proven to be effective, and which they are so well trained to offer?

In a recent overview of the research literature applicable to this discussion, Roger Greenberg observed: "Spending a few minutes with a patient and writing a prescription does not substitute for building a treatment alliance and inquiring about what is really going on in a patient's life." He went on to point out that a number of outcome studies comparing antidepressants to placebos showed there is very little difference. "The media and the advertising industry have greatly oversold the value of these medications by using such labels as 'miracle drugs' in their marketing campaigns."[3]

Citing numerous National Institutes of Mental Health and university studies, Robert Whitaker, a medical journalist, maintains that not only are anti-psychotic medications frequently ineffective but, over the long run, they may actually be harmful. He refers to other studies that have shown the newer, much more expensive 'atypical' anti-psychotic medications are essentially no more effective than the far less expensive earlier ones. He notes that these new medications, initially tested in clinical trials primarily by clinicians funded by the drug companies and yielding questionable results, now account for most of the drug company revenues. In his book *Mad in America* . . . Whitaker concludes that these drugs, therefore, are principally about profit rather than the best interests of seriously ill patients. He refers to a number of recent European studies demonstrating the efficacy of psychotherapy (psychologists take note!) with very judicious drug treatment as yielding substantially better results with "schizophrenic" patients than anything seen in this 'entrepreneurial' country.[4]

One may conclude, therefore, that any attempt at symptom reduction with drugs alone, without psychological exploration of the underlying factors and appropriate psychotherapeutic interventions, raises the likelihood of the need for a lifetime of medication for many patients.

Psychoactive medication, a cynical perspective

Psycho-pharma-pseudocals

Pharmaceutical companies have marketing departments whose job it is to develop names for prescription medications. I imagine the names they choose are expected to suggest their intended outcomes and facilitate their sale at unconscionable markups, 'buy'-products if you will. I have noticed that these appellations frequently overstate the effects and contribute to what can lead to an over-reliance on psychotropic medications.

One might allow a whimsically cynical look at the quest by psychologists for 'prescription privileges', assuming that despite their scientific training and exacting ethical standards they are able to put aside the tenuousness of the data supporting psychiatric medications as well as all the marketing exploitation involved. Known for their expertise in the understanding of semantic symbolism and the use of communication techniques, psychologists could develop their own classes of really expensive alternative medications with powerfully suggestive names that might turn out to be just as effective, given the equivocal science on which current psychiatric medications are based. Here are some suggestions:

Adament: enhances assertiveness.

Adavit: reduces dissociative feelings; gets you 'out of it'.

Addaroll: improves the productivity of bakers.

Afib: enhances truthfulness.

Avilify: ameliorates abusive and disparaging attitudes.

Axiom: helps you get back to basics.

Concretin: improves abstraction ability.

Empathin: promotes identification with the feelings of others.

Equinim: potentiates friendliness.

Frozac: an anti-depressant ice cream.

Indoorfan: reduces perspiration secondary to anxiety related to house arrest.

Lamental: ameliorates feelings of remorse.

Metamusical: allows one to go to, and at, a Broadway show.

Narcease: terminates self-centeredness.

Noprocrastin: intended to reduce procrastination but so far drug trials have been disappointing as patients have been putting off taking it.

Oxymoron: eases the pain of exposure to limited intelligence.*

Paradoxin: reduces stress associated with exposure to contradictory information. (Drug of choice for politicians and news reporters.)

Podium: improves mood stabilization during public speaking.

Proximal: reduces fear of intimacy resulting from crowded situations.

Prozaic: makes stressful situations seem ordinary.

*Prozetz***: facilitates martial arts training.

Reparation H: ameliorates a **H**istory of childhood angst.

Riddle-inn: enhances the puzzle-solving abilities of hyperactive children when staying at hotels.

Roladexedrine: energizes and focuses the search for contact information.

Standacyde: helps you get out of the way of other people.

Stellazine: facilitates understanding of the play, "A Streetcar Named Desire".[5]

Unsure: for those ambivalent about nutritional supplements.

---

* More precisely estimated if Howdull? is administered prior to IQ testing.

** Zetz. A strong blow or punch, Yiddish.

Vi-aggravate: facilitates sexual functioning in the face of extreme frustration.

Zoloftig***: used to treat plump women with depression.

Notes

1 R. Whitaker, and L. Cosgrove, *Psychiatry Under the Influence. Institutional Corruption, Social Injury, and Prescriptions for Reform*, New York, NY: Palgrave Macmillan, 2015.
2 Moses, 1391–1271, BCE.
3 R. P. Greenberg, The Return of Psychosocial Relevance in a Biochemical Age: The Register Report. *The Magazine of the National Register of Health Service Psychologists*, Vol. 40, Spring 2014.
4 R. Whitaker, *Mad in America, Bad Science, Bad Medicine and the Enduring Mistreatment of the Mentally Ill*, New York, NY: Basic Books, 2009.
5 T. Williams, 1947.

*** From the Yiddish word *zaftig* meaning a woman with a full rounded figure; plump.

Chapter 19

Health insurance abuses

Or unsurance?

Certainly everyone is entitled to make a living yet it has always seemed paradoxical that profiting from someone else's pain and suffering is considered an acceptable vocation, no matter how well-intentioned or committed the clinician. Despite its acceptance in our culture, the notion that pain and suffering can be ameliorated if one pays the financial price seems essentially to be exploitive and a fundamentally immoral practice. By progressively shifting costs to the consumers, health insurance companies have highlighted this issue and given it new meaning.

Instituting a single-payer, government-controlled system, with all practitioners on salary, would remove the profit motive and re-humanize health care, thereby eliminating the morally flawed system we have today. It would result in dramatic cost savings and make care universally available.

Here are two examples of defects in the current system: One morning I called an insurance company for clarification of a claim they had denied. After paying close attention to the phone menu "as it has recently changed", I finally reached someone name Brad who was extremely understanding and helpful, and sounded like a really nice guy. Brad said he would review the whole matter, most likely to my advantage, and I should call him back at 2:00 that afternoon. I did as he instructed, once again paying careful attention to their new phone menu. A woman answered and when I asked for Brad she told me, with obvious indifference, "Brad is no longer with us."

The next example: I once sent three claim forms, all in one envelope, to an insurance company. Two of the claims were paid rather promptly but when I subsequently called to inquire about the third claim, I was told they never received it. "But it was in the same envelope," I explained. Taking no responsibility for their oversight, they asked me to fax a copy of the 'missing' claim form, which I promptly did. Subsequently they informed me that I had submitted it too late for consideration!

Follow-up, through middle level managers who promised prompt resolution, yielded nothing but the eventual refusal to return my calls. I then wrote a letter to the president of the company, whose name and address were available only on their commercial website and nowhere else, and described this situation as well as a few others of a similar nature. I ended with an implied threat to take this to the state authorities if it was not resolved satisfactorily. Eventually this yielded an apology and payment, but perhaps it's really all about discouraging clinician participation in order to reduce the insurance company's overall costs; in this case, they accomplished that goal as I dropped any further participation with that company.

Then there was the insurance company that was paying psychologists the same $70 for 45 to 50 minutes of individual psychotherapy since they first began including psychologists, i.e. circa 1970. Recently, however, they actually *reduced* their hourly rate to $65! Certainly this is contrary to the concept of inflation.

Workers' Compensation reimbursement rates in New York have generally been higher than the reimbursement rate for other kinds of claims; the amount is set by the state. So it was with great surprise that I noticed an insurance company, one I had a standard contract with, had paid me less than half the amount I billed on a Workers' Compensation claim.

The 'Explanation of Benefits' (EOB) that accompanied the check informed me that I was being paid according to the contractual rate I had with that particular insurance company and *not* the Workers' Compensation rate. Having never encountered this 'sleight of hand' before, I called the insurance company for clarification. The person I spoke with confirmed that the payment was indeed correct, based on a provision *buried deep in my signed contract.* I then called the Workers' Compensation Board and spoke to a representative who confirmed this 'new development', and informed me this wrinkle would soon be spreading to other insurance companies as well. When I asked why clinicians had not been warned about this, there was no explanation and it was suggested I write a letter to the Chairman of the Workers' Compensation Board. During the course of this conversation I said if insurance companies are allowed to evade the state mandated rates, the Workers' Compensation rates would eventually be rendered meaningless. He agreed and suggested the only apparent remedy would be corrective legislation. (See "Advocacy" above, to recognize where that gets you!)

The procedure codes used on insurance claim forms were recently altered. For example, a code that previously referred to a 45–50-minute individual psychotherapy treatment time was inexplicably changed to only a 45-minute individual psychotherapy 'hour'. As a result, a number of insurance companies used this five-minute time reduction as the justification/pretext for dropping their fee for this service by two to three dollars, giving new meaning to the term 'rip off'.

Then there was the surely fictitious account of the oncologist whose wife had died of cancer. When asked how an oncologist could let his own wife die from a disease within his specialty, he replied he didn't accept her insurance! The irony of this fabricated tale serves to illustrate the corporate attitude that has taken over our current health-care system.

Chapter 20

Money inevitably drives policy

... and policy loses

During those halcyon days at the Community Mental Health Center, an eight-year federal grant covered the greater portion of our work. The grant ended in 1975 and although some state and city funding remained, massive layoffs resulted, leaving those affected individuals bewildered and demoralized. The following (excerpted) letter was sent to the hospital board of trustees requesting a meeting to discuss the matter:

> As a clinical staff, we see the proposed reduction in our staffing levels as dangerously impairing our capacity to provide adequate services for our community. . . . The abrupt and immediate termination of staff will mean that many patients will be denied the necessary opportunity to deal with and understand the loss of their therapists and some may even arrive at their appointments next week to discover the therapists are simply gone. . . . We understand that the major source of our difficulty is the city's unwillingness to provide the necessary funds. . . . We strongly suggest that both the city and the hospital rethink their financial priorities. . . . A hospital that has funds to build a new garage for staff parking should certainly be able to find money for salaries. . . . Our staff, as well as the (staff of the) medical center, has long been committed to a community-oriented practice of mental health. We feel it is imperative to take a stand at this time in order to preserve this important concept.

Not surprisingly, the requested meeting never took place, provoking a level of frustration that resulted in the brief takeover of the Community Mental Health Center building. As well, the hospital's CEO was taken hostage by a small subset of the staff, the angriest and most radicalized. This act was never forgotten nor forgiven and, of course, it accomplished nothing.

When business becomes intrusive and destructive

Fee for service via Medicare, Medicaid and private insurance signaled the death knell for community education and intervention, as these were no longer reimbursable services. Although some residual of the community mental health ethic remained, the business model that evolved over the next several years contained ever more complex regulations and increasing documentation requirements, designed apparently to minimize payment. We learned that 'money drove policy'; that budgets and regulations rather than clinical concerns dominated the dialogue; that if you didn't write it in the record, it never happened. Imperfect documentation became a justification for reduced or denied reimbursement for services even if those services had been correctly rendered. The quality and accomplishments of the staff were measured by what was written in the record, rather than the actual clinical treatments rendered. The mantra became: Do more with less.

In the very early days of electronic medical recordkeeping, in an attempt to cope with the economic pressures and create more time for direct patient care, I set about developing the clinical content for an electronic medical record (EMR). At the same time, I developed and implemented computer programs to facilitate tracking, recording and billing for hundreds of clinical patient services each week. Our new electronic medical record program was based on an extensive procedure manual[1] I had previously written.

After finalizing all of the comprehensive clinical texts for the templates, I suggested the hospital copyright the clinical content of the program, believing this to be a legal option as well as a good business decision. Nothing came of this, however, until some years later when we learned of new arrangements with the software vendor. It appeared the hospital had arrived at a preliminary understanding with the vendor and several hospitals in the state for a form of 'barter': The hospital's current psychiatric templates would be shared among these hospitals, with the vendor acting as a kind of broker. In return, the other hospitals involved would create various medical specialty templates that would also be shared.

In a meeting with department leadership I noted that, given their plan, all of our intellectual property, as well as that of the other hospitals', would become a part of the vendor's program, which *they* could then copyright and profitably sell to other hospitals. After a brief pregnant pause, there was an essentially non-committal response. No further discussion ever took place and the whole project eventually mysteriously vanished.

To everyone's initial satisfaction, greater efficiency and time-savings were realized in the transition from hand written records to computers. It wasn't long, however, before administrators and regulators saw how easy it was to add more questions to be answered, and fields to be completed, and record keeping in the EMR became increasingly time consuming. Eventually this led to a downward spiral in the quality of clinical services. Narrative accounts that previously had humanized the patient in the record gave way to expanding checklists that reduced patients to discrete bits of information in a non-integrated format. The constrictive nature of the choices for completion of the record led to mindless entries, and the staff needed to be constantly reminded: "The computer is not your brain!"

One might cynically speculate that the more time it took to complete the record, the fewer patients could be seen and billed for, thus the requirements actually were insidious cost-reducing measures for the regulators who were also the payers. Although the clinical service I directed was able to stay slightly 'ahead of the curve' through these EMR technical innovations, the overall long-term effect of moving toward a business model proved to be corrosive and destructive. The former sense of community and mission among the staff became, for the most part, just a memory.

In an Opinion piece in *The New York Times* in 2016, Robert Wachter, MD, Professor and Chair of the Department of Medicine at the University of California, San Francisco noted,

> Evidence mounted that even superb and motivated professionals had come to believe that the boatloads of measures, and the incentives to "look good", had led them to turn away from the essence of their work. In medicine, doctors no longer made eye contact with patients as they clicked away.

Wachter further pointed out that Medicare's acting administrator recently "announced the end of a program that tied Medicare payments to a long list of measures related to the use of electronic health records".[2] Quoting Andy Slavitt, Medicare's director at the time, Wachter noted: "We have to get the hearts and minds of physicians back."

How can you fault more information? An absurd but real case in point was the requirement to ask about the patient's 'spirituality': Circa 2002, I was a participant on a national accrediting committee where this requirement was one of the agenda items. Despite the 'evidence based' trend of the entire mental health field, none of the very experienced mental health professionals in that room (and, to my knowledge, no one since) has been able to define the meaning of 'spirituality' in measurable terms, and yet you will find this question currently mandated in hospital Electronic Medical Record.

An even more preposterous example of this type of over-regulatory syndrome took place sometime in the late 1990s at a meeting for health-care professionals in New York City. We were told that treatment pre-scriptions had to be very exacting in order to qualify for reimbursement. In particular, if group psychotherapy was prescribed, the name of the therapist had to be part of the prescription and, according to Medicare, if that particular therapist was absent and someone else led the group, there would be no reimbursement. Ridiculous but true! Out of sheer frustration with Medicare's deviation from common sense, a Kafkaesque requirement clearly designed to minimize reimbursement, we came up with an equally outrageous, fanciful but emotionally satisfying solution: All therapists would legally take on the same name, thus cleverly dodg-ing this stricture. Fortunately, this became unnecessary as the intense blowback from the mental health community resulted in the eventual withdrawal of this requirement.

The pressures to seize every single billing opportunity were enormous. Patients often waited on long lines at the cashier's window to obtain the receipts they needed to present to the clinicians they would be seeing. If they had no receipt, they were to be denied treatment no matter how urgent the clinical situation. As the supervisor, I was frequently dragged into this vortex of anxiety and found myself having to make the point by sardonically saying, "The only basis for treatment without a receipt is cardiac arrest! Severe bleeding is a gray area!!"

Souled out

As a result of the current business model diagnosis and treatment have, without a doubt, become incidental to fiscal solvency. The constant demand for 'maximum' productivity, measured primarily in financial terms, has created significant frustration for clinicians as they struggle to deliver complex services to increasing numbers of patients in a limited amount of time. This trend has finally reached its inevitable absurdity, as noted by *The New York Times* on January 18, 2018: At one specific hospital, and probably others, "physicians are repeatedly overruled by administrators" on admission and discharge decisions, "cherry picking cases . . . in order to improve metrics . . ., lift its quality of care ratings" and hence the "bottom line".[3]

In a subsequent article in June 2019, *The New York Times* reported: "One additional task after another is piled onto the clinical staff members, who can't – and won't – say no. . . . Primary-care doctors spend nearly two hours typing into the EMR for every hour of direct patient care."[4] *The Times* further noted the continually expanding power of administrators (read business-planners) by pointing out, "From 1975 to 2010, the number of health-care administrators increased 3,200 percent. There are now roughly 10 administrators for every doctor." Imagine the improvement in health-care delivery if the money invested in administrators had been directed at increasing the number of health-care providers and improving facilities.

A central but perhaps not so obvious question emerges: Why do public and non-profit hospitals have to 'make money' while this is not required of the military, police and fire departments, all providing vital services under serious and often life threatening conditions? Why is the direct provision of health care a commodity while the direct provision of military, etc. services is not? How did health care allow itself to be 'sold out' by business interests when the others have not? A partial answer is that many entrepreneurially oriented practitioners, along with the insurance and pharmaceutical industries, have historically (and profitably) monopolized control of the delivery of health care in this country. The service ethic has always been primary to military, etc. personnel in the performance of their duties, but today when it comes to health care it is secondary.

The New York Times has noted enormous and long standing health industry resistance to health-care coverage for all: "Doctors, hospitals, drug companies and insurers are intent on strangling Medicare for all before it advances from an aspirational slogan to a legislative agenda item."[5] Until some form of publicly funded universal health care is developed in this country, just as we have publicly funded the military, etc., money will continue to drive policy and remain the principal concept directing patient care.

Notes

1 M. Heinrich, *Documentation Procedures, Policies and Guidelines* (Unpublished), 2005.
2 R. Wachter, How Measurement Fails Doctors and Teachers. *The New York Times*, Sunday Week in Review, January 16, 2016.

3 D. V. A. Philipps, Doctors Say Rating Push Hurts Medical Care, *The New York Times*, Vol. CLXVII, No. 57, 829, January 1, 2018.
4 D. Ofri, Is Exploiting Doctors the Business Plan? *The New York Times*, June 9, 2019.
5 R. Pear, Eager to Sink Medicare Plan, Lobbies Unite, *The New York Times*, Vol. CLXVIII, No. 58, 248, February 24, 2019.

Chapter 21

Escalating administrative control

All's well that Orwell

This leads to what is perhaps a futuristic yet imaginable speculation: Might the next technological advancement be the requirement that every clinician wear a Bluetooth earpiece, complete with a mini-microphone and camera? By means of this device, all clinical sessions could be fed back to a central server and, using voice recognition and voice-to-text software, the session could be downloaded right into the electronic medical record. This would have the distinct advantage of reducing documentation time, allowing clinicians to see even more patients per day. Thus the essence of a 'drive-thru' treatment session would be approached and could possibly end with: "Do you want fries with that?"

But it gets better (or worse, depending on your perspective). This model could be interactive, that is, the clinician could be monitored in real time by supervisors who would offer clinical directions or, as part of the overall trend toward more and more efficiency at the expense of quality clinical work, the clinician could simply be told when enough has been done for that particular individual, to wrap it up and move on to the next double-booked patient. One can even envision insurance companies hacking into this system in order to 'authenticate' billing claims.

And, only conceivable today because of National Security Agency (NSA) revelations, there would be the requirement that this device be worn throughout the day (they'll know if you take it off) with the understanding that even private conversations would be monitored, thus minimizing open staff dissent in a facility, or even the time honored pasttime of making fun of supervisors. Theoretically, the bathrooms would be blocked, but only theoretically. Hard to imagine? Think of where we were only ten years ago with regard to technology and privacy, and note this quote from a *New York Times* article in 2014: "The use of video monitoring – covert or disclosed, of patients or providers – has proliferated as high-quality, inexpensive technology has become increasingly accessible."[1]

I had direct experience of the positive potential of a lower tech version of such monitoring when I observed an uncooperative patient being forcibly carried from the inpatient dining room by four nursing assistants, one to each limb, all the while complaining that her knee hurt. The assistants finally deposited her in the hall in front of her room and continued to surround her until the treating resident arrived and ordered them away. I happened along at that moment and the resident and I were able to calm the patient and encourage her to move into her room and onto her bed. The follow-up investigation included review of extensive video footage from the numerous cameras in place. Both the abusive as well as therapeutic aspects of the treatment of this patient were revealed. Many of the corrective decisions that stemmed from this incident were based on observations from those tapes.

In September 2014 an article in *The New York Times* stated: "The New York City Police Department will begin equipping a small number of its officers with wearable video cameras. . . . 'It is the next wave,'" Police Commissioner Bratton said.[2] Currently all uniformed patrol officers have been equipped with body cameras.

As imagined above, one might anticipate a similar "wave" seeping into mental health care.

Notes

1 T. A. Lahey, Watchful Eye in Hospitals, *The New York Times*, Vol. CLXIII, No. 56, 415, February 17, 2014.
2 J. D. Goodman, City Police Officers Will Start Using Cameras in Pilot Program, *The New York Times,* Vol. CLXIII, No. 56, 615, September 5, 2014.

Chapter 22

Mostly business, most of the time

Mini-malism

As a result of an imminent change in the reimbursement policies of various insurance carriers, a large municipal hospital system recently decided it had to reduce the average psychiatric inpatient length of stay to just 12 days. Ideally getting patients out of inpatient units more quickly is a good thing, when motivated by the desire to improve the overall care. In this instance, however, it was clearly for economic rather than clinical considerations, just another example of money driving policy.

Among many 'innovations' intended to expedite achievement of this goal was the requirement that large white boards be displayed on the inpatient units indicating the length of stay and planned treatments for each patient. It was hoped more rapid progress toward discharge would be achieved by publicly creating not-so-subtle pressure on the staff. They were told that "of course" clinical judgment and ethics should prevail in any given case and, in the event of a clinical error as a consequence of this plan, they were assured the administration would support them; no one seriously believed that. The message was clear that any staff member whose ethics and judgment sustained an unacceptably high average length of stay would find himself or herself under review. As evidence of this trend throughout the health-care field, a *New York Times* article from January 2014[1] described a threat to terminate physicians who did not maintain emergency department admissions quotas.

While it is desirable to minimize the length of inpatient stays, it is difficult to see how this stress-inducing and demoralizing policy could have any lasting positive outcomes. Based primarily on financial considerations, with no scientifically derived clinical basis, and lacking the availability of sufficient outpatient services including day treatment, the result could spell little more than eventual disaster for many patients.

In order to put this questionable initiative in the best possible light, leadership sent an open letter to the staff:

> The challenging economic realities of today require a more cost efficient approach to psychiatric inpatient care without sacrificing quality and outcome. This essentially provides us with both a stimulus and an opportunity to significantly revise and improve this care. It will necessitate our making full use of our skilled and proficient interdisciplinary teams using collective input to produce comprehensive treatment plans in order to accelerate the discharge process to greatly expanded ambulatory follow up.[2]

There are times when a patient truly needs long-term care as in the case of a young man resistant to short-term medication and psychotherapeutic input. His symptoms of severe chronic psychosis included poorly controlled and disorganized behavior rendering him exceptionally vulnerable out on the streets. Although he was often transferred to a state hospital for extended care, invariably he would be discharged within a few weeks, apparently just as disturbed as when initially admitted. Outpatient treatment was not realistic for him because he just couldn't get there. Out of desperation, his mother actually chained him to the radiator in her apartment as the only means she could see to protect him.

The urgency for rapid (and clearly inappropriate) discharge on the part of the state hospital is ironic in view of the state's long history of having retained thousands of patients for up to 30 years to life (also clearly inappropriate). Obviously neither extreme is acceptable or compatible with quality care. With tongue in cheek, one can only speculate that if there is any embarrassment on the part of the state with regard to lengths of stay, these excessively reduced ones perhaps bring their historical statistical average (ignoring the substantial standard deviation involved) more into line with acceptability.

Another example of premature discharge of a patient from a state hospital involved the patient referred to our day treatment service with, as it turned out, a significantly incomplete history. Had we known all the details we would likely have declined the transfer but it wasn't until after the patient's suicide that we learned of his extensive history of impulsivity and violence, not only at the state hospital but also prior to his admission there. Despite the fact that his drawings contained very violent themes, in his short tenure with us he evidenced no display of such behavior. Better treatment? Less controlling environment? Hard to know! But a complete initial history, given that patients in day treatment are not constantly observed, might have prevented his death.

A columnist in *The New York Times* reported:

> More than half of prisoners in the United States have a mental health problem, according to a 2006 Justice Department study. . . . In 1955, there was one bed for every 300 Americans; now there is one for every 3,000 Americans. . . . Taxpayers spend as much as $300 to $400 a day supporting patients with psychiatric disorders while they are in jail. . . . For some the only place to get help for a mental illness is behind bars.[3]

A month later *The New York Times* reported:

> Corrections officers have struggled with an increasing concentration of mentally ill inmates who experts say often respond defiantly or erratically to the harsh, zero tolerance disciplinary measures successfully employed in the past . . . (and the) over reliance on solitary confinement and force . . . perpetuated violence among inmates, particularly the mentally ill, who have crowded the nation's correctional facilities as mental hospitals and other institutions have closed.[4]

In a follow-up article, the same writer noted that New York City Council members finally acknowledged the city's inadequate mental health system: "As mental hospitals have closed in recent decades, an increasing number of people with mental illness have ended up in jails."[5] He went on to quote a city councilman as having said the jails are being used to provide mental health services that should be provided by mental health facilities. This was dramatically demonstrated by the above account of the patient chained to a radiator by his mother for his own protection; clearly he required admission to the state hospital even though it lacked, and continues to lack, sufficient beds and staff to meet the need for sustained care of the seriously and chronically mentally ill.

Limiting the availability of treatment may appear to have reduced the overall cost of mental health care, but, in fact, the costs to society have actually gone up due to the resultant incarceration of so many mentally ill, at far greater expense. The best guess about manipulated, reduced lengths of inpatient stays and the current limited availability of outpatient services is that administrators anticipate numbers alone will measure their individual success. Given their personal ambitions, they may seek even further reductions in care. Perhaps this is the goal they are headed for: 'The patient will be younger upon discharge.' But, just perhaps, that might be an exaggeration!

Notes

1 J. Creswell, and R. Abelson, Hospital Chain Said to Scheme to Inflate Bills. *The New York Times*, Vol. CLXIII, No. 56, 391, January 24, 2014.
2 M. Heinrich, *Open Letter to the Staff*, May 8, 2013. Reluctantly written, for leadership upon their request.
3 N. Kristof, Inside a Mental Hospital Called Jail. *The New York Times*, February 9, 2014.
4 M. Schwirtz, Rikers Island Struggles with a Rise in Violence. *The New York Times*, Vol. CLXIII. No. 56,445, March 19, 2014.
5 M. Schwirtz, Council Sees Flawed Mental Health System. *The New York Times*, Vol. CLXIII, No. 56, 454, March 28, 2014.

Chapter 23

Administrative abuses of power

Petty mal treatment

As well as witnessing the current model in health care (and elsewhere), where policy is being driven by money, we are seeing an increasingly dysfunctional and disrespectful upper level management attitude toward clinical staff. The abusive use of power has turned the mental health system into something akin to 'futilism'.[1]

Recently, at one municipal hospital organization, a directive from top level management to all staff acknowledged the possibility that increased workloads would result from anticipated budget reductions, and made a commitment to support, improve and re-humanize the health-care environment for all.

Encouraged by this communication, the psychiatric department staff raised concerns about the impracticality of their increasing workloads, the result of recent resignations of significant numbers of disaffected staff necessitating the assignment of ever more cases to the remaining staff. Apparently experiencing 'cognitive diffidence' (as opposed to the better known concept of cognitive dissonance), department leadership initially ascribed these complaints to 'lazy workers' resistant to change rather than taking steps to make corrections consistent with the directive. When specific complaints of humiliation and denigration of the staff as well as increasingly unrealistic demands for excessive workload productivity were presented to the department leadership, their proposed solution was that staff should see patients less frequently and/or for less time at each session. Of course the upsurge in an already excessive documentation burden was ignored, as was the likelihood that more frequent hospitalizations would result. This recommended 'speed-up' also created a risk that significant violations of regulatory procedures, professional standards, guidelines and ethics could occur. What a great model we were demonstrating for the students! After all, we weren't just making donuts here!

The 'cognitive diffidence' prevailed. When a mid-level supervisor was insulted and urged to resign by an upper-level manager, the outpatient staff was catalyzed. They filed a complaint with the administrators of the entire municipal hospital system and demanded a meeting to voice their complaints about the onerous requirements being placed on them, as well as the increasingly demeaning style of leadership. In particular, the level of disrespect shown to psychiatrists by administrators was remarkable. Where's psychiatric élan when you need it?

Eventually, however, what seemed to be a serious investigation was initiated by the human resources department. Many professionals on staff at the time, as well as some who had already resigned, (and even a few who had been driven out) were interviewed. Comments allegedly made by human resource administrators conducting the inquiry included: "It seems like you are all telling us the same thing about the problems . . .", "What do you think we should do with these people . . .", "Something should happen within a few weeks."

Several months later the investigation was concluded but then, ironically, people from the very same leadership group that had been the target of the investigation were the ones who finally promised some change! No announcement was ever made, but a consultant (actually an 'executive coach') was brought in presumably to 'coach' these managers into being actual leaders. Sadly, no discernable changes resulted despite leadership and team-building meetings. The real issue, specifically those leaders with their dysfunctional management styles, was bypassed! It appeared that this 'executive coach' did not concern himself with systems issues, for if he had he would have noticed that this particular department was made up of three relatively separate and poorly communicating entities, i.e. the clinicians, the nurses and the administrators, each engaging in a 'parallel play' approach to daily operations. Unclear lines of authority and accountability made it difficult to create or modify programs, or to give clear direction to subordinate staff. Those leaders with personality and/or competence issues remained in place and, one by one, staff members found their own ways to solve the problem, either by leaving or just keeping their heads down, constraining their effectiveness in order to preserve their jobs.

This same large municipal hospital system had previously initiated a top to bottom reorganization following a model initiated by Toyota USA, and referred to as "Lean".[2] This was their attempt to make the organization more efficient and effective. Yes, they understood "Patients weren't cars". Major claims were made for "Rapid Improvement Events" and "paradigm shifts" and total involvement of all employees in the problem solving process. Their vision was of a "transformed" system, a public hospital system in which everyone was a 'problem solver', every employee was valued and contributed value to the system. They claimed the concept of "Transformational Leadership" was central to their goals: "Transformational leaders lead by example, challenge workers to innovate to the point of changing the environment, and achieve organizational change through inspiring and coaching workers."[3]

Well, given the rather tragic and discouraging account of what transpired with staff complaints as noted above, where were these "Transformational Leaders"? Where was the "every employee valued"? If 'paradigm shift' actually does happen, it didn't happen here.

Workplace ambience has been devolving. Yes, staff dissatisfactions, vying factions and political, philosophical and ideological struggles have always existed, but never before was there such palpable fear, the feeling that everyone involved, at both management and staff levels, was constantly being devalued. As professionals who once believed we were rendering essential human services requiring the assumption of significant levels of responsibility for making difficult and independent judgments, we were now being forced into more mechanized and rigidly prescribed approaches to our work.

A growing mistrust of the system has gradually diminished self-esteem, imposed chronic anxiety and taken a substantial emotional toll. How can staff hope to sustain quality care for their patients when faced with a sense of their own imminent and ultimate irrelevance? This can be summed up by the title of Richard Farina's memorable novel: *Been Down So Long It Looks Like Up To Me*.[4] In essence, when a bad situation continues for a long period of time, it often becomes the norm.

In my judgment, and consistent with the expressed ideals of "Lean", the critical functions of management are to sustain realistic goals and support staff. It may be that only by continuing to challenge management practices will we ever see a return to rational, humane leadership and well-run clinical environments, where universally enlightened quality care that values the well-being of patients and staff over all else, is provided. That will be the day when, once again, **policy drives money!**

De-mensche-a*

During the many years I directed clinical behavioral services in a department of psychiatry, my overriding (and frequently met) objective was

* Derived from 'mensche' – Yiddish for human being. In this case, dementia!

to shield clinical practice from bureaucratic administrative rigidity. My challenges to the practice of arbitrary bureaucracy and its impact on clinical practice were not without cost; on more than one occasion they resulted in personal attacks against me.

One example is the way in which I was informed of my promotion to a rather substantial clinical directorship. First my attention was drawn to the many enemies it was claimed I had made over the years, and then to opposition from certain administrators to my advancement. Walking out with this new, if slightly tarnished promotion, I was uncertain if I had actually been advanced or merely reprimanded. But this was only 'foreploy'!

Later came yet another example of authoritarian abuse, a demonstration of how a relatively small issue could become magnified and over-personalized. In my role as director of the unit, I had assigned a small office to a part-time staff psychiatrist. Although he found the space perfectly acceptable for his work, when upper management in the department learned of this office assignment they perceived it as disrespectful to a psychiatrist! We were both called to a meeting where we were subjected to vicious personal attacks over this essentially trivial matter. At a time when there were really significant problems facing the department, they ordered me to assign him a larger office, one more befitting the privileged professional status of a psychiatrist. Having no recourse but to comply, at the close of the conversation I cautioned that a repetition of such flagrant abuse of power would result in a formal grievance to hospital administration.

An incident of even greater import, one involving improper documentation in medical records, took place at a meeting in the office of upper level management. Up until that time the staff of my clinical service had consistently been following the documentation guidelines given to us by the department of psychiatry but, now for the first time and in the presence of the entire psychiatry leadership group, we were rudely informed those guidelines were incorrect! Consultants hired to protect the department from potential conflicts regarding Medicare regulations advised that not only could Medicare demand to be reimbursed for our improper documentation, but we could also be arrested for fraud! Obviously that specter made hospital leadership extremely nervous since Medicare had recently cited a number of programs similar to ours for committing fraud. So, despite the fact that my clinical staff had been following what we only now were being told were incorrect regulations, they had done so in keeping with the hospital's instructions. Despite the logic of our defense, hospital management held us responsible for this 'error' and, with sweeping blame and blatant disrespect, disregarding the professional credentials and collective experience of the staff in the room, declared we were all "inept". An administrator from outside the department was selected to supervise all of us going forward. Although perceived (and certainly intended) as an insult, we nevertheless made it work and successfully sustained our reimbursement rate as, after all, wasn't it really just about the money?

Still, residual blame persisted and a sacrificial lamb or scapegoat (animal of your choice) was required. Without warning I was called into my supervisor's office and told:

> It is my unpleasant duty to inform you that I am demoting you from your current position as director.

Stunned, I asked for a rationale but received only references to vague, anonymous complaints made against me over the past several months. No details concerning persons or incidents were provided, thereby effectively denying me any opportunity for rebuttal or correction. When I countered that I had recently received very positive feedback from the supervisor responsible for overviewing documentation corrections and updates, I had always had excellent annual evaluations and my service consistently received high ratings from city and state accrediting agencies, his response was only silence.

That evening, however, he called me at home and said: "I've considered your criticisms with reference to my not bringing these matters (still unspecified) to your attention and, therefore, I am rescinding the demotion." As far as anyone else was concerned it never happened.

My next performance appraisal was very positive albeit with an implication there had been some (never specified) fault on my part:

"Both I and all others to whom I have spoken are highly complimentary of the way in which you accepted the criticism and went about raising the standards of your performance to its present high level."[5] Just another example of management covering its own ass!

Then came the day when department leadership was replaced by a far younger, financially-oriented group that appeared completely devoid of any of the human warmth once associated with mental health professionals. The downward slide toward my own departure began soon after.

State funding for day treatment services was being drastically reduced at that time and, as a consequence, the decision was made to significantly downsize the day treatment service I had been leading. This meant that someone with my credentials and experience was no longer needed and my current salary was no longer financially sustainable. Instead, they offered me the directorship of an even larger service, one that was in great financial and administrative difficulty, and in need of what they then considered my "expert leadership". Instead of being gracious with their proposal, however, they told me I could either accept what they presented as a promotion or resign from the hospital, a peculiar way to acknowledge an individual's value to the institution. They gave me a year to turn around this service and even promised a bonus upon the successful outcome. I chose to accept their offer because, at the time, it seemed a challenging opportunity.

Immediately I assessed the issues and began implementation of a rather complex recovery plan. Imagine my surprise when, within six weeks of starting in this position, they summarily informed me that the hospital budget could no longer sustain this service and my mission now was to be its complete dismantling. They expected me to divide the remaining personnel (after layoffs) into two smaller clinics serving the same patient population, but with much narrower service mandates. I was to direct one of these. Unmistakably, this was money driven administrative manipulation that victimized many, and likely was developed in advance of my appointment, given the limited time frame for this entire venture.

For the next half year I successfully directed this small clinic until a new decision was made to integrate it into the general outpatient department and, once again, my services would no longer be required. Despite my extensive and very successful leadership history, they now offered me a position where I would be teaching and supervising psychology interns and psychiatric residents 14 hours a week, at a per diem rate. I recall facetiously saying at the time that a year hence I would be called to a similar meeting and asked if I would be interested in working in the mailroom.

It turned out I wasn't far off the mark. Barely eight months into that position I was again called to a meeting and rather offensively informed by leadership of the department that I was being paid at an "incorrect" salary level. Had I not been so taken aback by this remark I might have said, "Oh, that's okay, you're paying me enough," but of course that wasn't what they meant. And then, despite my long association with this department, they actually referred to me as an "outsider," and curtly informed me that as of the beginning of the New Year, merely one month hence, my hourly *per diem* pay would be reduced by about 50%, and, over the first few months of the New Year, my time would be reduced to only two hours a week. My supervisory work was to be assigned to others, with lesser qualifications and experience, thus saving money for the department. (Quality? What's that?) Never for a moment was any concern expressed about how this short notice might affect me financially or otherwise. Despite the medical center's economic problems, here in the considerably spacious office in which we were sitting I could see about $10K worth of recently purchased furniture, prompting my reflection that the only larger room in this hospital was the one for improvement.

This finally was the ultimate and intolerable insult, not only to me but also to the patients and staff I worked with. After several decades of what was indisputably exemplary service, my 'soft' layoff was being initiated, with merely one month's notice. In retrospect, I can see that the progressively focused and personalized process that began with what now seems a contrived promotion, was just a preliminary step toward my eventual exit while still allowing them to capitalize on my skills and experience to close down a service they no longer judged to be economically or clinically relevant.

In my letter of resignation, effective in 30 days, I explained I was doing so with sadness and deep regret that my work was no longer considered of value. I sent copies to the hospital's executive leadership, naively hoping an inquiry into this demeaning treatment might be made since I was aware of similar complaints lodged by others who had also provided long and quality service to the institution.

Instead, my computer access was immediately shut down and I was ordered to a meeting with department and hospital management where I was told I would be paid for the next month but I was not to return to work. I told them it had been my intention to use the last month to make appropriate professional transitions and bring closure to my relationships with the residents and interns whom I had been supervising. That was of no interest to them. Although the primary emotion I expressed in my resignation letter was sadness, they chose to designate me an "angry employee" and I was 'graciously' ("we won't need security guards") given assistance with the immediate removal of all my belongings from my (now former) office.

Not surprisingly, the hospital's executive leadership, clearly a party to this farewell, never responded to me.

Given the overall number of terminations before and after mine, one might speculate whether the mental health center leadership was trying to build a substantial alumni association, or were they receiving kickbacks from neighborhood restaurants catering all the inevitable goodbye dinners? Maybe both.

Notes

1 An allusion to feudalism, a social system that ended in the 1400s: In exchange
   for protection, serfs and vassals served under the lord in their wars and farmed
   their lands.
2 J. P. Merlino, J. Omi, and L. Bowen, eds., *Lean Behavioral Health*, The Kings
   County Hospital Story: Oxford University Press, 2014.
3 Ibid.
4 Penguin Twentieth Century Classics, 1966, New York, NY.
5 Performance Appraisal, October 11, 2000.

Afterword

An alternative to current amoral imperatives

As said by Robert Whitaker in *Mad In America*,[1] "any close examination of our care today should give us pause." Business interests and the increasing medicalization of behavioral health treatment seem to be competing for the dehumanization of the patient.

In our supercharged economic environment, given the systemic injustices I have described, why would anyone want to remain in this uphill struggle to render compassionate treatment to the mentally ill? This question is a serious one, especially for those of us who have had lengthy careers in the field and can remember better times, those of us who retain a passion and the capacity for this work and who feel we still have much of value to offer. Speaking for myself, I feel a moral imperative to continue my efforts to reclaim a policy balance that will enable the next generation to expect and be able to offer more humane treatment.

Appundix

Recognizing its protective value, throughout my career I have used humor when trying to cope with all the contradictory forces surrounding me in my quest for logic and quality clinical policy and application. The pun, in particular, has been a saving grace as it immediately alters the context and direction of a conversation. Puns (and other humorous remarks) can dissipate frustrations and sometimes even disarm the opposition.

To quote James Geary,

> When you make a pun, you bring together two distinct ideas – a coincidence of sound, significance, or meaning – and a realization results – Punning folds a double knowledge into words. To make and understand a pun, you must grasp two things at once: the primary, apparently intended import of a word or phrase, and the secondary, usually subversive one.[2]

In my experience, this has been especially true during tense moments, for example during clinical and administrative meetings, when humor often puts important points into sharp, resolving relief.

So, while one should not put all of **ones' egg samples** in one basket of puns, here are some I have accumulated over my career:

Roughly clinical

Amelio-rate – the cost of a psychotherapy session.

Annualism – having a stroke once a year.

Backteria – a place where chiropractors eat.

Defecation – can't hear shit.

Ego scout – someone looking for lost identities.

Endorphanage – where happy kids await adoption.

HIPAA-campus – where the brain pun center is probably located.

Homeopathic panic – what happened when he took a trace amount of a certain remedy.

Narcolexia – falling asleep when reading.

Penis envoy – an ambassador who is a dick.

Remorse Code – a way to express your regret.

Sibling robbery – one sister stealing from another.

The first sign of *'demensia'* is misspelling it.

There was a neurologically impaired art therapist who couldn't *draw* a conclusion.

My mother-in-law said she liked to sleep in the *fatal* position.

He had more *flaws* than the Empire State Building.

He was *hampered* by his dirty laundry.

An older person who is dizzy may be having *'many-years' disease*.

Psychiatric diagnosticians are *mental detectors*.

I've had an amputation he said *off handedly*.

Then there was the architect diagnosed with an *out of building experience*.

Would you prefer music *or-castration*?

I think I'm menstruating she said *periodically*.

His pornographic poetry sold for $5 *per verse*.

'Erection' is a word comprised of *phallic syllables*.

He was a masochist who had *PMS envy*.

Viagra is *pubic assistance*.

The tailor ironically had *pressing* problems.

The psychotherapist wanted to talk about *resistance* but I didn't.

He made hostile humorous remarks during sex until he experienced a *sarcasm*.

If someone murders a person with a multiple personality disorder does that make him a *serial killer*?

Showered with emotion there was not a *dry towel* in the house.

Podiatrists drive *tow trucks*. They don't foot the bill, they *bill the foot*.

Having lost his job, the jockey became emotionally *unstable*.

She became pregnant on the *sperm* of the moment.

Belching and flatulating simultaneously raises the risk of creating a *vacuum and being crushed to death by negative air pressure*.

Her parents were separated when she was 4. Someone finally threw a *bucket of cold water* on them.

Roughly non-clinical

Backhoe – someone who accepts payment for anal sex.

Bar 'mitzvah'[13] – buying a drink for someone who desperately needs one.

Blintzkrieg – attacking someone with a thick pancake filled with cream cheese or fruit.

Catalyst – an itemization of cows in my herd.

Condom-minion – 10 Orthodox Jewish men with prophylactics.

Context – a book used in a prison.

Confusion – prisoners sticking together.

Condescending – a prisoner walking down the stairs.

Decapitated – the kind of coffee Marie Antoinette and Anne Boleyn drank.

Egg is stenchal – how a rotten egg smells.

Eggnostic – one who doesn't know which came first.

Falsehoods – headcover worn by fake Klansmen.

Fauxplay – pretending to arouse someone.

First Served First Come – an advertising slogan for a brothel.

Forepay – paying a hooker in advance.

Freelance – how an unarmed knight might work.

Impasta – a type of fake spaghetti.

Inter mittens – those worn occasionally.

I tend to use the word '*binge*' excessively but hardly ever use '*infrequent*'.

Life is a mixed bag and some are *left holding it*.

Malapropism – an airplane in a lot of trouble.

Peruse – a South American country where people spend considerable time very carefully looking over things.

Proselytute – a religious missionary.

Pussyeebo – a blow up doll.

Rip on – when you are given too much change.

Shtupgart – a sexual German city.

Stationary store – much easier to walk into, isn't it?

Wouldn't touch that with a 10 ft. pole or a *short Hungarian*.

Acronym, Ohio.

Then there was the army band that only played **pla*tunes***.

She filed her nails *alphabetically*.

You can *armadillo* but you can't make it fight.

Orthodox women were fighting for the right to *bare arms*.

How about the luncheonette supply company that was *counter productive*.

Feeling milked by the situation, he was *cowed* by its *udder* nonsense.

Crossing your fingers makes it hard to put on gloves.

I don't like pets he said *dogmatically*.

He was so depraved he should have worn *ethical breeches*.

He had a very bad *fall*; it got cold so quickly the leaves never turned color.

A musical quartette is *four-play*.

He was cooking on the *grill* of his dreams.

Nearing your house is experiencing *imminent domain*.

How about an *In Your Face Book* for people who mainly want to insult each other.

It's rusting he said *ironically*.

Have I seen a medium? No, but I've seen a *large*.

He'd have one more drink and that would be the *last of the Mojito's*.

The gay guy who just got a *mandate*.

The cheap hooker *nipple* and dimed him.

There was a riot in the kitchen and *pan-demonium* broke out.

A peaceful person will *pass-a-fist*.

The plumber had a *wrenching* experience but it was only a *pipe dream*, which gave him a *sink*ing feeling. He woke up *drained and flushed*.

Sacred and *propane* – that's a gas.

He was so into dried grapes that it became his *raisin d'etre*.

I'd better change the tire he said *sparingly*.

Having fallen off the horse, he was *saddled* with the realization that it *behooved* him to know getting back on was *insurmountable*.

You can *testimonial* but will it pass?

You can *tortellini* but you can't see it all in one day.

He was so unattractive he couldn't even *turn on a stove*.

Did you hear about the librarian who was *working off the books*?

His sports car was so fast that when you stepped on the gas *you got younger*.

The escaped prisoners were found, by the guards, encased in ice. Before acting on any plan, they had to consider the *frozen cons*.

Unintended political slogans: *Free Will!* ... *End Construction!* ... *End Road Work!*

And finally, a note about another dysfunctional work situation: One day I noticed a small industrial building that housed a business called 'Ed's Welding'. A seemingly clever advertising slogan came to mind but I never got around to bringing it to Ed's attention. Sometime later I noted the business was gone. My slogan: *'All's well that Ed welds!'* [4] I could have saved Ed.

Finally, a psychiatric treatment that makes cents![5]

Notes

1 Whitaker, R., *Mad in America, Bad Science, Bad Medicine and the Enduring Mistreatment of the Mentally Ill*, New York, NY: Basic Books, 2009.
2 J. Geary, *Wit's End: What Wit Is, How It Works, and Why We Need It*, New York, NY: W. W. Norton & Company, 1st edition, November 13, 2018.
3 Hebrew: among several meanings the term *mitzvah* is an expression of human kindness.
4 With apologies to Wm. Shakespeare, *All's Well That Ends Well*, 1605.
5 Photograph taken on Warren Street, Hudson, NY, June 16, 2014.